Hubbell Sea Captains

by Hilbert R Hubble

Published by
The Hubbell Family Historical Society
Marjorie M K Hlava, President
2017

ISBN 0-9623097-6-1

Correspondence may be addressed to:

Hilbert Hubble
2900 N. Leisure World Blvd #411
Silver Spring MD 20906

Printed by:
Lulu.com

Preface

I was first attracted to this subject when I noted the large number of Hubbell hits in "shipping news" while researching old newspapers. These papers reported the departure and arrival of vessels, usually giving the ships name, captain's name and port where they departed from or where they are sailing to. There are many, many ships with the same name and usually only the master's last name was given.

My interest was piqued during several visits to the Mystic Seaport located within easy distance of my daughters' home in Rhode Island. During a recent visit to New York City I was walking along the Skyway when I noticed the old Star Line pier, still waiting for the arrival of the TITANIC. Later, during a cruise around Manhattan, I noticed the large number of abandoned piers. What stories these piers could tell! How many Hubbell masters tied up here? Were there Hubbell's waiting for the arrival of cargoes, with large investments at risk? More recently, (2010) an 18th century ship was unearthed at the World Trade Center.[1] What made this ship so valuable is that it is a unique example of a common, utilitarian vessel; the kind our ancestors sailed. By the time the Hubbell Family Historical Society held their reunion in Mystic, I was hooked.

What drew these Hubbell men to the sea? The master (captain) of a ship was an honorable, prestigious position and it did not matter how large the vessel. Life at sea was dangerous and many seamen perished but the rewards for a few were great. Nearly every New England family felt the influence of the sea trade. As Lewis G. Knapp noted in his *Stratford and the Sea* "The seas were full of Captain Hubbell". Therefore, it is fitting that we try to understand more about the trade and the conditions that carried our ancestors to the sea.

One of the first settlement tasks was to build boats for fishing, communication and trade. As a result, the ocean became the economic mainstay of Connecticut. Ships were the only practical means of transport, there were no conveyances capability of carrying heavy loads over the primitive roads. New England became a center for ship building owing to the availability of cheap timber, and the many rivers with access to the sea.

---

[1] New York Times, 30 July 2010, *"A Workhorse of a Vessel that Helped Build the City"*.

Preface

Shipyards were on the river banks, and moved upstream as the supply of timber gave out. Commerce was brisk, notwithstanding the rocky coast and severe winter weather. Nevertheless, Connecticut became a major shipping center conveniently located between the major ports of Boston and New York.

The purpose of this study is to document the Hubbell men and woman that depended directly on the sea for their livelihood, and the events that influenced their lives.

The following are acknowledged for their help and assistance: Janet Stewart at newsbank.com, Immigrant Ships Transcribers Guild, The Library of Congress, the David Ramsey Map Collection, the Rutherford B. Hayes Presidential Center, the Mystic Seaport, Library and Museum, the Godfrey Library, Pat Dawson at the Hubbell Museum and Library, and Early American Newspapers, an Archive of Americana Collection, published by Readex (Readex.com) a division of NewBank, Inc. for newspaper images.

The author is a retired Naval Officer with degrees from Chaminade University, Central Michigan University and the Naval War College. He has over 30 years' experience researching the history of one of North American's earliest families and has published "A Military History of the Hubbell Family in North America", and most recently the" Millennium Edition of the History and Genealogy of the Hubbell Family". He lives quietly in Silver Spring, Maryland with his wife of 59 years Joan.

A can bouy on the beach compared to the size of a man standing next to it
Figure 1 - publicdomainvectors.org

Introduction

The research for this book took many twists and turns and was complicated by the maritime intelligence gathering of the past. The first data point for a commercial voyage was an advertisement announcing the name of the ship, the ship's captain, a departure date, destination, and location (wharf, pier, etc.). While very useful, advertisements in newspapers were only available for a very small number of trips. Some examples of advertisements are reproduced throughout this book. The departure date was flexible depending on the accumulation of cargo. At some point a decision was made to sail, permits were obtained and fees paid. Clearance was granted by the port authorities, routinely reported in the papers and this provides the next data point. Although cleared for sailing, the actual departure depended on weather and the tides. The difference between "cleared" and "sailed" could be days. For example:

> CLEARANCES
> Ship, Citizen, Hubbell, Havannah.[2]

From this we know the type of vessel (Ship), the name of the vessel (Citizen), the surname of the Captain (Hubbell) and the destination (Havannah). We also know that the ship and cargo are in place and ready to go.

Once the ship sailed and was lost from sight, nothing could be known about the precise location of the vessel until it either was sighted at an intermediate anchorage, encountered a passing vessel (who then reported the sighting when next in port) or arrived at the destination. Our experience with instant communications makes it hard to imagine going for days, weeks or even years (China voyages) not knowing if your vessel was still afloat and her cargo safe.

In the case of the coastal trade, the arrival at an American port was duly noted in the local papers and quickly (within a day or two) the information was available to the owners and other interested parties.

---

[2] New-York Gazette and General Advertiser 7 February 1796.

Introduction

Custom House, New Haven, Octo. 15, 1772
ENTERED IN,
Sloop Swallow, Hubbell, from Boston.[3]

From this we know that the Sloop Swallow under Captain Hubbell has arrived at New Haven on the 15th of October 1772 from Boston. The Captain had to pay all necessary fees before the vessel could unload her cargo.

Ship News
ARRIVED, DAYS
Brig Independence, Hubbell, Exuma 36[4]

In this case we find out that the voyage from Exuma (Bahamas) to New York took 36 days.

In the case of overseas ports, if the arrival was noted in local papers, those papers had to be transported back to the United States and the papers may be weeks or months late. The most common source of arrival information was from Captains who noted in their logs the ships in port, when they arrived, where the ships were from, how many days at sea and the master's name. Occasionally the cargo was mentioned. When the reporting Captain arrived at his home port, the information was collected from his logs and reported in the papers.

COMMERICAL MARINE LIST
SINCE OUR LAST
Ship Severn from Canton- . . . Sept 11 on the outward passage in the straights of Sunday (between Sumatra and Java ed.), fell in with the Catherine Ray, Hubbell, from New York for Canton . . .[5]

This report was 7 months old but may be the first news the owners received. Additionally, the Captains logs often reported on political situations, prices, disasters at sea and war progress.

---

[3] Connecticut Journal 16 October 1772.
[4] Commercial Advertiser 18 November 1801.
[5] Commerical Advertister 16 April 1804.

Introduction

FROM HAVANNA.

Charleston, Feb 8.

By the arrival of the Schr, William Hull, capt Hubbell, we learn, that accounts had been received there from the British army, near New Orleans, to the 17th of January. They confirm the news which had already reached us from other quarters, of the complete defeat of the British on the 8th ult. . . .[6]

Contemporary newspapers are a trove of information about our early Hubbell sea captains. However, the information provided was often limited. For example, early maritime reporting by newspapers gave either the name of the vessel or the captain, not both. Later reporting was more complete. Also, the data used for this book was limited by the availability of extant newspapers. Many were lost; consequently the data for a particular voyage may be incomplete. Last, and most vexing is the fact that the Captain's Christian name is rarely given. Unless otherwise noted, all ships mentioned in this book are under Hubbell (various spelling) masters. Enjoy!

---

[6] Daily National Intelligencer 21 February 1815

Introduction

Table of Contents

Chapter 1

The Beginnings for the Hubbells

The high seas are a distinct kingdom where the captain is king. He has supreme authority, literally over life and death. Time and space are different from the land since the nearest port could be days or even months away. Over the years, special maritime laws were enacted to give him that authority since land laws are useless at sea. And just a few pieces of wood separate the crew and passengers from certain death.

Most merchant ships carried a master known as the Captain, one or two mates who were in charge of steering and navigation. Ships on long voyages may need specialists such as carpenters and coopers. The bulk of the crew were ordinary seaman, usually very young. Learning navigation was the route to advance from ordinary seaman to mate. For the coastal trade this may have consisted of learning various landmarks, for the longer voyages, knowledge of the celestial navigation was essential. Although some ship owners and masters used slaves as crewman, I found no direct evidence that Hubbell's used slaves in their crews.

While we know the names of the Hubbell Captains, there is another group of Hubbell's who went to sea as part of the crew. For these Hubbell's there were many hardships. They were usually quite young and separated from any social or psychological support in their home. They worked in an environment where they were bound by law to obey the will of the captain and if they did not there were harsh punishments. Additionally, they had no control over who they associated with both on and off duty, or where and when they would go. To top it off, they earned the lowest wages of any American worker. This is in stark contrast to the popular conception that going to sea was somehow romantic.

The life of a crew member in the day of sail was difficult. Watches were 4 hours day and night, the provisions were salted, risk of physically injury was high, and they were often subjected to tyrannical officers or just incompetent ones. On the other hand although the risks were great, the rewards included adventure and opportunities coupled with long periods of boredom at sea. Quarters were cramped since valuable space was saved for the cargo which made money for the investors. Food was usually poor, and the crew lived in a never completely dry environment, and whatever the

1

Chapter 1

weather, the ship had to be sailed. It was very dangerous to be aloft in heavy weather. Oilskins were used to protect the seaman from the weather but the men lived in wet clothes; and fresh water could be a problem. It has been estimated that at one time one out of ten persons of New England were associated with the maritime life. [7] The relatives of crew members that died at sea or in a foreign port may never be notified. An exception is the case of Ira Hubbell (1427[8], 1802-1862) son of David (547) a seaman on the Bark ALMERIA out of New York, a report was filed with the State Department that he died in Shanghai, China 29 May 1862. The government requested that the *Boston Daily Advertiser* publish the report his death for 3 days[9].

With marine insurance, merchants were fully compensated for their losses and were never personally at risk. However, merchant seaman risked impressments, occupational hazards at sea, and pay was not increased as profits increased for the merchants. The crews risked the most and were paid the least.

The earliest settlers of New England colonies were probably not ship wrights or sailors, but they had to learn to build the vessels necessary to transport products and to fish while other settlers learned to sail these early crafts. Shipbuilding was the earliest industry in America requiring the use of many different skills. We know that vessels were built by and for Hubbell's but we lack sufficient details. Fortunately the New England coast featured bays, natural harbors and resources to support ventures to sea. When and how the Hubbell family became first involved is hidden from us but it safe to assume that the experience of Richard Hubbell travelling from Britain to Connecticut influenced his perception of the importance of the sea. Surely his grandchildren, especially those who became Sea Captains, heard the story of Richard Hubbell's (1, 1625-1699) three thousand mile ocean crossing. One can only imagine facing a two to three month trip at sea and all the potential dangers. The recent discoveries of four New England graves in the Republic of Suriname shed some light. The seafarers were buried far from home on the Paramaribo River from 1758 to 1765 and include sea captains from Middletown, New London and two from Newport. This former Dutch colony consisted

---

[1] Albion NE p 43
[8] The first number in these references refers to the individuals number in the Genealogy of the Hubbell Family, the second numbers are the birth and death years
[9] Report of American Consol at Shanghai, 7 Aug 1862

Chapter 1

of sugar plantations using slave labor and was part of the Triangle Trade[10].

The earliest settlers found that the natives conducted their commerce by water in birch bark canoes since only narrow trails existed for land communications. Movement inland was restricted by the thick forests and settlers were already looking to the sea for their survival. However, the early European settlers had a recent sea experience during their transport to New England and that, coupled with the need for commerce with other settlements, probably led to early construction of sea going vessels. By the time Richard Hubbell arrived, there were already thriving settlements on the coast and the first American vessel had been built some 30 years earlier. About the time Richard arrived, the colonists had moved beyond coastal fishing to the abundant banks of Newfoundland.

Connecticut was in a potentially favorable location between the excellent harbors of Boston to the north and New York in the south. In 1702 there were 8 lawful ports in Connecticut, including Stratford, and an office was established for entering and clearing vessels called a Naval Office. The Long Wharf in New Haven existed as early as 1644[11].

Weather is always a factor in New England with summer afternoon winds and fog and winter with cycles of freezing and thawing. Ice forms rapidly on the rigging of vessels and blocks the harbors. Gales with driving winds and wet snows reduce visibility. The challenge of New England weather required particularly hardy sailors.

The English colonies were a source of great wealth for Great Britain. The essentially English population would naturally desire products of the home land and willingly export the raw materials to support a closed mercantile system. The Navigation Acts provided the framework for commercial operations. The acts provided that all trade within the empire was to be conducted in either English or colonial vessels. These vessels had to be built and owned in England or America and their masters and three-fourths of the crews were English or American. Additionally, certain valuable produce could only be exported to England and English products could only be

---

[10] America and the Sea pp60-62
[11] *Hartford Courant* 2 Jan 2012.

3

Chapter 1

imported through England. This list of valuable produce rapidly expanded. In return the colonies gained the protection of the British Navy, readily available credit and an exclusive West Indies market.

Vessels were built in the colonies cheaper than in England and ships built of hard wood, abundant in the American forests, lasted longer.

The earliest commerce consisted of fish, lumber etc. from New England to the West Indies and return of molasses, rum and sugar. Along the Atlantic coast, the Connecticut farmers shipped grain to the New York market.

The resources of the American continent were worth fighting for and gave American merchants opportunities to profit by supplying the army with provisions and munitions. Additionally, many ship owners developed their own private warships called privateers. I have not found any evidence of Hubbell owned privateers although we do know of one armed vessel.

Prior to the French and Indian war of 1754-1763, little has been found regarding our Hubbell's and the sea. The earliest newspaper account was noted in the *Boston Gazette* of 9 June 1747 which reported the capture of a "sloop from Stratford in Connecticut bound for Antiqua, Ezra Hubbell, master" was captured by a "Spanish privateer of 12 carriage guns and 70 men belonging to Havanah, Signor Joseph Alvertes, Commander." After removing most of her lading, she was given back to the crew and they arrived safe in New London on the 19 May. Obviously a vigorous West Indies trade was already in existence by the time of our first reports. Ezra Hubbell (73, 1716-1758) was the grandson of Richard Hubbell (1) and the son of Peter and Katharine Wheeler Hubbell (19). He was 38 when captured and had just started his family, their first child, Isaac (245, 1746/7-1787) was born the year before[12].

In the *Boston Evening Post* of 9 May 1748 "Custom-House Boston ... 7 May ... Cleared out, Hubbell for New York". The same paper on 4 July 1748 Captain Hubbell was noted arriving from New York and departing for New York on the same day and later in the month he departed for Connecticut. The Sloop CATHERINE made one of the earliest recorded voyages from Boston to New York and returned

---

[12] *Boston Gazette* 9 June 1747.

to New London in May and June 1748 under command of Ezra Hubbell (73).

The following year, the *Pennsylvania Gazette* reported Captain Phineas Hubbell (a314[13]) arriving from Barbados, West Indies in the sloop FREE MASON. Phineas was born about 1727 and married Elizabeth Reeves 14 December 1741 at St Michael's Parish in Bridgetown. A total of four voyages to and from Barbados were reported[14].

The sloop JANE & SARAH was sailed from Barbados to Philadelphia by Phineas Hubble in September and October 1746. See also FREE MASON above.

"Yesterday arrived here the Sloop Jane and Sarah, Captain Phineas Hubble, from Barbados. On the 15th instant, in the Evening, about 15 Leagues to the Southward of Cape Henlopen, he saw a Sail, which came up with him about 9 at Night, and proved to be a French Privateer Schooner, whom he engaged for about an Hour and a Half, with his People on board; in which Time he hulled her several times, and supposes he put her on the Careen for near two Hours, After which she bore down on Captain Hubble again, which so intimidated his Men, that they all took to the Boat, except a Passenger, who seeing the Captain resolved to fight the Vessel as long as he could by himself, came aboard again out of the Boat, and said he would stand by him. Accordingly, the Passenger steering the Vessel the Captain fought his Guns most bravely and successfully for above an Hour, and at last obliged the Frenchman to sheer off. On the 17th he met with Captain Grant from Georgia for this Place, who spared him some Hands, a Sail, and what other Things he wanted, to repair the Damages his Vessel and Rigging had received, and did not leave him, till he saw him safe within Cape May.[15]"

One of the earliest indications of the coast trade and incidentally the only reference seen to Zachariah Hubbel (23, 1694-1751?) who would be 57 years old and whose date of death is unknown, is reported below. Fisher's Island is at the eastern end of Long Island Sound, off the coast of Connecticut and 8 miles from New London. The shallop is a heavy boat usually with 2 masts with fore and aft lug sails and/or oars. The shallop is designed for and used in shallow water.

---

[13] An "a" proceeding a number indicates an unplaced Hubbell

[14] Phineas is probably not a direct descendant of Richard Hubbell, our immigrant ancestor.

[15] *Pennsylvania Gazette*, 23 Sept 1746.

Chapter 1

"Taken up adrift in the Sound, to the Westward of Fisher's Island, eight days ago, by Capt John Rudyard, from Annapolis-Royal, and carried into Oyster Bay, a small shallop of about 10 tons, having a great quantity of earthen ware on board. She had both cables out, but no Anchors, and is supposed to have drove out of some Harbour. By papers found on board, the Master's name is Zachariah Hubbel, and belonged to James Ingram. Whoever owns the said shallop, by applying to said Rudyard, at Oyster Bay, proving their property, and paying the charges may have her again.[16]"

A sloop (no name given) arrived in Philadelphia 13 December 1753.

"In the thick Weather on Friday lasty Captain Hubbel in a Sloop, bound in from Antiqua, ran on the East Bank; the Crew got all safe ashore but the Vessel now lies in such a Condition, that it is thought almost impracticable that either she or the Cargo can be Saved[17]"

After these early beginnings, the reports of Hubbell sea going activity becomes more detailed.

UNNAMED VESSELS

Some early reports gave the Captain's name, without a ship's name. A very early example is Ezra Hubbell and his voyages in a sloop from Stratford to Antiqua and New London from 3 May 1746 to 19 May 1747. See page 4

---

[16] *New York Gazette*, 7 Oct 175 .
[17] *New York Mercury*, 10 December 1753

Chapter 2

The Seven Years War and the Growth of Seaports

At the end of the 7 years war, England was the preeminent sea power and American commerce depended on the protection of the British Navy.

During the war years of 1775-1783, little shipping news was reported in contemporary papers as commerce was at a standstill. It wasn't until 11 October 1783 that reporting on shipping resumed with the Naval Office of the Port of Boston reporting the arrival of the sloop JULIUS CAESAR under the command of Captain Hubbell of Connecticut. It was during this period that the growth of New England seaports was seen. In contrast to the large commercial ports of Boston and New York, the seaports of Connecticut became specialized as a result of active commerce and trade with the West Indies. New Haven, New London and Stonington had deep water harbors and river ports such as Middletown and Norwich reached into the interior for agricultural markets.[18] Many cargos of grain from Connecticut farms were carried by our Hubbell captains. New Haven had a waterfront with warehouses, wharfs and featured Long Wharf that reached far into the harbor (extended in 1810). In 1784, about 30 New Haven vessels were engaged in coastal, West Indies, and weekly packet trade. Ancillary trades supported the shipping industry with rope walks, sail lofts, carpenters, blacksmiths, and the ports provided recreation for the crews.

Figure 2. Port of New York, Currier and Ives, Library of Congress, Governors Island in the center.

---

[18] Albion p 47.

Chapter 2

Before we delve into the activities of our Hubbell sailors we need a word about the family left behind. The role of woman in the sea faring culture has not received much attention. Page 102 of *America and the Sea: A Maritime History* discusses the Women of Nantucket and their uncommon responsibilities while their husbands were at sea. Responsibilities that often included running their husbands businesses during long absences. Income was probably sporadic for these wives while their husbands were at sea and many became widows at an early age owing to the dangerous occupations of their husbands. Many found other ways to supplement their income: *The New York Mercury* published an advertisement for sword fighting lessons at the home of widow Hubbell by the ship yard.[19]

The period 1754-1763 (7 Years War) saw the first rather complete records for our Hubbell Captains. In 1759, Captain Hubbell was observed arriving and departing New York and Connecticut but no Christian name or name of the vessel. In 1761, the *New York Gazette* reported the DISPATCH, a sloop out of New York cleared 28 September 1761 for Monto Christo (Monte Christo, Haiti) under the command of Nathaniel Hubbell (396 ?-?) the son of Asa Hubbell (126) and Anna Bloomfield. The sloop RANGER, Nathaniel Hubbell master arrived in New York on 27 July 1767 14 days out of Saint Croix (U.S. Virgin Islands). He was mentioned as a sea captain in the 1995 *Additions and Revisions to the History and Genealogy of the Hubbell Family* (A&R) and undoubtedly many of the voyages with unidentified Hubbell captains belong to him.

Another active captain was Josiah Hubbell (69, 1736-1795) another grandson of Richard. The SEA FLOWER was a 57 ton sloop built in Milford, Connecticut in 1763, and her master Josiah Hubbell conducted regular trade between Boston and Connecticut from May 1763 to May 1769. The sloop was a lightly designed vessel with a single mast and two sails. The sail before the mast was called the foresail and the one aft of the mast was the main sail, often on a boom.

Captain Josiah Hubbell continued his coastal business in the SEAFLOWER from Newfield to Boston and later he was the master of the SWALLOW, a sloop of New Haven. She made the New Haven to Boston run from June to December 1772. He was also a member

---

[19] 9 October 1758.

Chapter 2

of a committee to obtain relief for the people of Boston as a result of the Boston Port Bill. He committed to transfer donations to Boston as proclaimed on 14 December 1774 in Guilford, Connecticut. On one trip, the donations transported by Captain Hubbell for Massachusetts Bay included 10 bushels of rye and 6 bushels of wheat.[20]

The VIRGIN, a sloop under the command of D. Hubbell, probably Dennis (121, 1743-1786), son of Captain Eleazer (25, 1700-1770) entered into New Haven 14 December 1769 from Saint Martins, a French and Dutch island in the northeast Caribbean Sea.

The sloop JULIUS CAESER (first with that name) was built in 1782 at Bedford, Massachusetts. She is described as 65 tons, length 52 feet 4 inches, draft 5 feet 5 inches, beam 19 feet inches with a single mast. Richard 3rd (24, 1696-1787) & Amos Hubbell (117, 1746-1801) were listed as owners and Amos and Ezekiel Hubbell (515, 1768-1834) as masters. On February 20, 1783 under the command of Amos Hubbell, she attacked and captured the British privateer THREE BROTHERS.

"Captain William Johnson (formerly of Guilford) in the service of the enemy commanding a sloop of 50 tons, and about 20 men was taken of Milford last Friday, and carried into Fairfield, by Capt. Amos Hubbel, of that port, in a sloop of about the same burthen, with 4 Carriage guns, and 60 men, 40 of them continental soldiers. Capt. Hubel, after receiving one broad-side, which did him no injury, returned it with a general discharge of musketry, which killed Johnson, and wounded 23 of his men, one of them named Hotchkiss, said to belong to Chesire, since dead. British privateer THREE BROTHERS. The prisoners are sent to Head-Quarters."[21]

On 12 October 1791 the sloop THREE BROTHERS touched at New Haven from Martinico (Dominican Republic), Captain Hubble.

Amos Hubbell (117), great grandson of Richard was heavily engaged in the sea going trade as fighting captain, master, builder and conductor of West Indies trade.

"Amos built a wharf near foot of Bank Street where he built 1 ship and 2 brigs for himself. However, his commercial business was not generally successful."[22]

[20] Knapp p 69.
[21] *Salem Gazette* 13 March 1783.
[22] Orcutt, p 70

Chapter 2

When Amos died, he owed about $9,000 dollars and a real estate auction by the Probate Court was held to raise the money to pay his creditors. His assets included 8 parcels of land from 6 to 65 acres and property in Bridgeport that included valuable buildings, lots, house, barn, wharf and stores.[23]

The sloop KINGSTON arrived in Philadelphia 1 July 1756 from Jamaica (British colony, now independent), Eleazer Hubbel (120, 1739-1810), master.

Voyages under Captain Hubbell were made from Boston to Connecticut and return from 5 August 1758 to April 1762. At least 21 voyages have been recorded but neither name nor type of vessel was noted. Most likely, the master was Josiah Hubbell (69).

During this period, American commerce was controlled by the legislators of England but they also enjoyed the protection of the Royal Navy. This was about to end.

Cockspur Lighthouse on the south channel of the Savannah River
Figure 3. publicdomainpictures.net

---

[23] *American Telegraphe* 19 January 1803.

Chapter 3

American Independence
1764-1783

British power was highest after the Seven Years war. Not only preeminent on the ocean, but Britain colonies in the New World expanded in the former colonies of France and Spain. At the conclusion of the war, Americans were proud to be part of the world's greatest empire that brought them prosperity and protection.[24] Although separated from the British Empire by the Atlantic Ocean, there were such strong commercial ties that Britain became dependent on her American and West Indies colonies as markets for her manufactured goods and for imports.

This dependency on her colonies bought attempts to raise revenues by a series of unpopular acts; acts whose impact fell primarily on the American seaports. These acts included the Sugar Act, Stamp Act, Townshend Act, and Tea Act. The seaports also contained the symbols of imperial power that proved to be the targets of resentment as well as the means of communications. The symbols included the admiralty courts, troop garrisons, and customhouses. The communications were achieved through newspapers, readily available news from "outside" and meeting places.[25]

To be fair, the British were trying to improve a system that saw widespread evasion of duties, ineffective enforcement and confused policy. The Americans could understand these attempts to improve commercial conditions but London was facing large war debts and an expanding colonial area to police. The prevailing British sentiment was that the colonists should pay for their own defense.

The Stamp Act (1765) extended to America an excise tax already in use in Britain. All legal documents were subject to these new duties and impacted heavily on the maritime community. Commerce relied on a large volume of documents; insurance, registrations, duties, bills

---

[24] AATS p.110
[25] Ibid p 111

Chapter 3

of lading, contracts etc. all requiring an official stamp that had to be purchased. In spite of widespread protests we can still find our Hubbell ancestors engaged in seaborne commerce. For example, the SEA FLOWER a 57 ton sloop built in Milford 1763 with master Josiah Hubbell conducted regular trade between Boston and Connecticut from May 1763 to May 1769.

The 13 ton schooner NEPTUNE (2) was built in Fairfield 1765, master Isaac Hubbell. She entered in New Haven on 23 June 1768 from New York and cleared for New York.

The sloop RANGER, Nathaniel Hubbell master, arrived in New York on 27 July 1767 14 days out of St Croix.

"The same day Capt Hubbel arrived here 14 days from St. Croix, on the 15th inst at Lat.36 he spoke Capt Miner, in a sloop from St. Croix bound for New York"[26]

The VIRGIN, a sloop under the command of D. Hubbell entered into New Haven 14 December 1769 from St Marti.

Possibly the SEA FLOWER or the SWALLOW under Captain Hubbell made the New Haven to Boston run at least 15 times between 1770 and 1773. Captain Josiah Hubbell was the master of SWALLOW, a sloop of New Haven. She made the New Haven to Boston run from June to December 1772. This was during a period of relative calm until the famous Boston Tea Party, December 16, 1773. As a consequence, the port of Boston was closed to all commerce, not just foreign, but coastal as well.

When the break with the British came, the Continental Congress passed a rule of no intercourse intended to punish the Crown, and the British passed the Prohibitory Act which removed the colony from the protection of the British Navy and prohibited trade. There are no newspaper accounts of Hubbell vessel arrivals or departures from 1772 to 1787. At various times, the major ports of Boston and New

---

[26] *New York Mercury* 27 July 1767.

Chapter 3

York were occupied by the British. Trade with the West Indies was very risky since American vessels were subject to seizure by the patrolling British Navy.

Many Captains turned to privateering but no record has been found of a ship under Hubbell command. Some Hubbell's must have signed on to privateers or the Navy. Samuel Hubbell (178, 1750-1807), of Southwark Town, Philadelphia was the son of Samuel (43) and Abigail Sterling Hubbell and served in the Revolutionary Navy in the brig LEXINGTON, Captain Henry Johnson. Samuel was taken prisoner 19 September 1777 and committed to Old Mill Prison near Plymouth, England 1 October 1777. He was pardoned for exchange 11 December 1779. Although signing a House of Lords Petition of June 1781 for exchange & release, he attempted escape, was re-taken and put in the "black hole" (solitary punishment) 6 July 1781 until July 29. He was still in prison April 1782.[27]

Now that they achieved independence, American merchants, mariners, and the government had to construct a new system of trade and protection.

Boston Seaport

Figure 4. publicdomainevector.org

---

[27] Kaminkow.

Chapter 4

The Articles of Confederation era (1784-1789)

When hostilities ended between Great Britain and her colonial colony in America, maritime merchants expected a golden age of commerce. Because of heavy investment in war time bonds, the merchants lacked the capital to replace lost and worn out vessels. The instability of forming a new government, the departure of loyalist merchants, and the war time debt combined to further reduce capital investment in shipping. The most damaging blow was the new commercial policy of Great Britain which deprived the new United States of America of all trade with British colonies including the West Indies.. The shipping interests now relied on non-British colonies and the coastal trade. New overseas markets in the Far East were on the horizon.

The PHOENIX a schooner of 34 tons was built in Dartmouth, Massachusetts in 1787 and registered 17 February 1802 in New York. She cleared Boston for Connecticut on 21 May 1787 and cleared New Haven for Boston 21 June 1787 under Captain Hubbell.

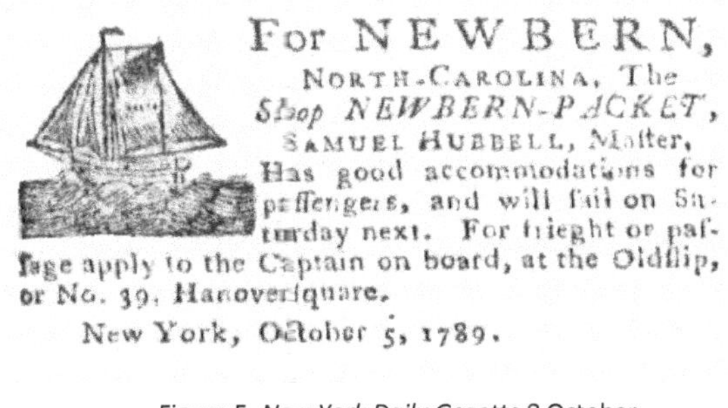

For NEWBERN,
NORTH-CAROLINA, The
Sloop NEWBERN-PACKET,
SAMUEL HUBBELL, Master,
Has good accommodations for
passengers, and will sail on Saturday next. For freight or paf-
sage apply to the Captain on board, at the Oldflip,
or No. 39, Hanoversquare.

New York, October 5, 1789.

Figure 5. *New York Daily Gazette* 8 October 1789. From Early American Newspapers, an Archive of Americana Collection published by Readex (Readex.com), a Division of NewsBank, Inc.

The sloop NEWBERN-PACKET, master Samuel Hubbell (177, 1750-1807) arrived in Philadelphia from Cape Francois (Haiti) 21

April, 12 June, and 25 August 1789. She then commenced a run from New York to Newbern, North Carolina in September and October.

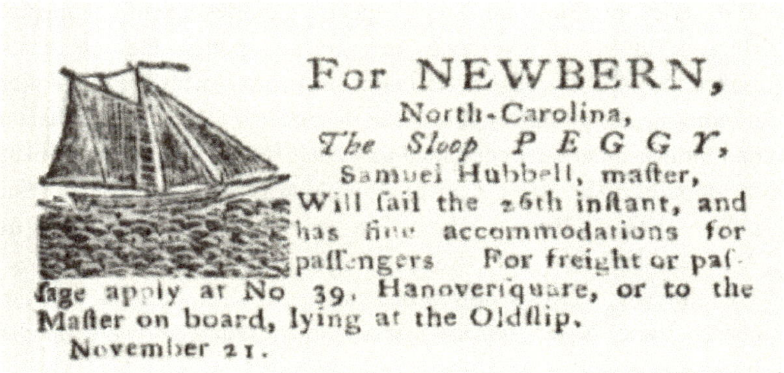

For NEWBERN,
North-Carolina,
The Sloop P E G G Y,
Samuel Hubbell, maſter,
Will ſail the 26th inſtant, and has fine accommodations for paſſengers For freight or paſ-ſage apply at No 39, Hanoverſquare, or to the Maſter on board, lying at the Oldſlip.
November 21.

Figure 6. *New York Daily Gazette* 26 November 1789. Early American Newspapers. op. cit.

PEGGY (1) a sloop sailed from New York to Newbern, North Carolina 26 November 1789 under Samuel Hubbell. She made three additional trips in 1790, under Captain Hubble.

The sloop INDUSTRY (1) first recorded in June 1787 when she cleared for North Carolina. She arrived in New Bern with 175 loafs of sugar, 1 cask and 25 gallons of Lisbon wine, sundries growth and manufactured goods of the United States and 858 bushels of corn. She made at least 7 more trips between July and December 1787.

The merchants Stevens & Hubbell was located at 145 Water St., near Crane wharf, New York City in 1786. The firm arranged for freight and passengers to Wilmington, North Carolina on the sloop PATIENCE and for Kingston, Jamaica on the ship COMMERCE. The firm dissolved 1 January 1787 owing to the indisposition of Mr. Hubbell and Ebenezer Stevens, a general in the Revolution, continued as Stevens & Connolly. The business consisted of a lumber yard, charter freight and passage. The firm continued for 80 years as Ebenezer Stevens' Sons.

Chapter 4

A contemporary Currier and Ives print (Figure 7) gives an impression of the large number of piers and shipping in the port of New York.

Figure 7. Currier & Ives from Library of Congress P & P collection 3e41602u

The partnership of Richard Hubbell (24) and Amos Hubbell (117) dissolved May 1795. They were involved in the merchant trade with the West Indies from 1783 to 1787 in business with son Amos under Richard Hubbell & Son coastal trade with Boston – Newfield, now Bridgeport Connecticut. Ezekiel Hubbell was the master on ships owned by Richard and Amos. After dissolution of the business in 1805, Amos built a "Yellow store" above the lottery bridge in Newfield and ran his own West Indies trade until he died in 1801.[28]

The new government recognized the need for regulation of the sea trade and administration of fees and duties as a source of government income. But now the income stayed at home.

---

[28] Knapp p120

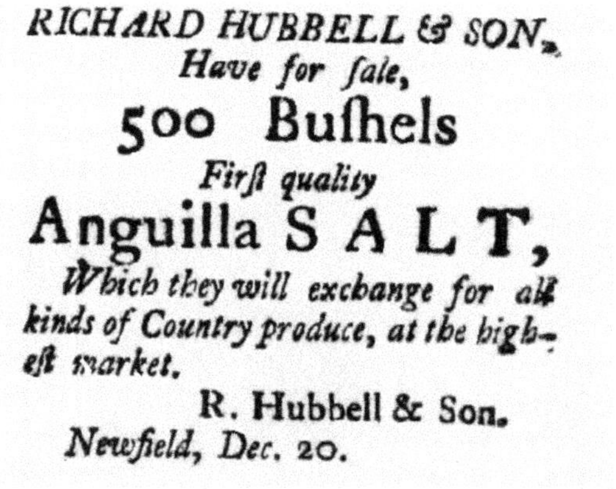

RICHARD HUBBELL & SON,
Have for ſale,

5oo Buſhels

Firſt quality

Anguilla S A L T,

Which they will exchange for all
kinds of Country produce, at the high-
eſt market.

R. Hubbell & Son.
Newfield, Dec. 20.

Figure 8. *American Telegraphe* 20 Dec 1796, Early American Newspapers op.
cit.

UNNAMED VESSELS (2)

Another early example provides the Captain's last name but no first name
or ship's name, or ship type. These particular trips occurred between 23
April 1748-26 September 1748 on a regular basis between the ports of
Boston and New York. Master's name Hubbell.

Chapter 5

The New Republic and a New Constitution

The period between the Articles of Confederation and the War of 1812 saw the Constitutional Convention and new regulations for the conduct of commerce. The first tariff of 1789 discounted by 10 percent all foreign goods that were shipped in American vessels and the tonnage act of the same year established duties for vessels entering American ports. All vessels engaged in foreign trade were required to be registered.[29] The regulations differentiated between coastal trade (Chapter 6), China (and European) trade (Chapter 7) and West Indies trade (Chapter 8). These acts also established a Customs Service and there are references to Salmon Hubbell, collector.

This period also saw a rapid grown in American overseas trade in all size vessels. The vessels sailed by our Hubbell ancestors became more specialized and were constructed of wood, with masts made of single large trees. The masts supported sails made of canvas that were sewed in large sail lofts. Cordage, including lines, cables and hawsers were made of many strands of fibers and twisted together to obtain the necessary strength. Smaller vessels were produced in shipyards on the banks of rivers that provided access to the sea and to plentiful lumber. The Connecticut River is a typical site providing the raw materials, labor and ocean access. Larger ship yards were established close to the mouth of the river or in protected waters in ports. A whole industry evolved to support the maritime trade, supplying the raw materials of wood, copper, cloth, and fiber and the finished masts, spars, fittings and cordage. Skilled carpenters, sail makers, and blacksmiths were needed to build and repair the vessels.

Brigs had two masts with square sails on both masts and typically displaced between 100-300 tons. Schooners had two or more masts of equal height or sometimes the aft mast was larger. A schooner was common in the coastal trade, and sailed with a smaller crew than a

---

[29] Labaree p. 167

Chapter 5

square rigged ship of the same size. Ships had three or more masts mounting square sails on each mast. Generally ships displaced more than 250 tons. Sloops were the smallest vessels used in commerce and had a single mast with one foresail forward of the mast. A sloop of 30 tons would have a typical crew of 5 or 6 sailors.

The port cities continued to grow in response to the rapidly growing trade. Docks, piers and wharves were often privately built and charged a fee for their use and waterfront property rights were uncertain. The adjacent streets were lined with wooden sheds and storehouses. The dock areas were crowded and ramshackle with carts, horses, baggage, passengers, cargo hawkers, money houses, stores, and warehouses.

John Lambert, a British visitor to New York in 1807 described the port. He said *there were bales of cotton, wool and merchandize, barrels of potash, rice, flour and salt provisions; hogsheads of sugar, chests of tea, puncheons of rum, and pipes of wine, boxes, cases, packs and packages of all sizes and denominations strewed upon the wharfs and landing places, or upon the decks of the shipping. All was noise and bustle. The carters were driving in every direction, and on board the vessels, were moving their ponderous burdens from place to place.*[30] *At the wharfs ships lined up sometimes 2 deep, the narrow waterfront streets were full of commercial buildings and warehouses lining one side belonging to ship owners, merchants, traders, and insurance agents.*

This period also saw a rapid expansion of Hubbell family merchants in the sea trade.

The firm Bedient, Kimberly & Hubbell was noted in New York 1795[31] . Bedient & Hubbell operated from 1800 to 1803 at 194 Water St., New York, with partners John Bedient and Walter Hubbell (504, 1767-1803) the son of Gideon Hubbell (160) and Sarah Wakeman. Walter Hubbell was as an employee of Bedient, Kimberly & Co when he married his second wife, Ann Law. The firm of Bedient, Kimberly & Co. dissolved 1800 to become Bedient & Hubbell and Walter became a partner. Their counting house at 194 Water Street

---

[30] Homberger p57
[31] *Evening Post* (NY)

Chapter 5

was between the Beckman & Burling wharfs. The partners leased and sold ships and cargoes. For example, they purchased the ship HURON at auction from the United States Government for $10,650 December 1800[32]. They were heavily involved in the trade with North Carolina, at one time wanting to lease 2 or 3 ships for that trade in tar, turpentine and occasionally flax seed, wheat, and black eyed peas. During the 28 months that the partnership existed over 79 ship arrivals in 53 different ships and as many captains were noted. The firm was very fortunate in that there was only one disaster at sea; the schooner BELL under Captain Tallman with a cargo of naval stores was stranded near Egg Harbor. The vessel was lost but most of the cargo was saved and brought to town in lighters. However, the seizure of the schooner TWO BROTHERS was a total loss. (see page 21 . The firm had facilities in New York and Brooklyn. When they moved from 194 Water Street to 85 South Street they moved their store and counting house which fronted about 60 feet. At the time of Walter's death, the Brooklyn facility consisted of store houses, docks and wharfs located near the ferry. Walter Hubbell died September 1803 and firm dissolved. By 1807 John Bedient was bankrupt and insolvent.

At some point, Walter Hubbell moved to Windsor, North Carolina and established the firm Walter Hubbell and Company in partnership with John Bedient. Windsor was on the headwaters of the Albemarle Sound on the Cashie River. By 1800 Windsor was in inland shipping center with landings extending two miles along the river. It was a logical port for the substantial trade between New York and the naval stores of North Carolina. Walter's estate was probated at Windsor with references to his wife Mary and one-half ownership of the cargoes of the Schooners ANTILOPE and JOHN.

A single reference to the firm of Greene & Hubbell of New York was found when the ship REBECCA under Captain Richards was cleared for Jamaica in 1811.[33]

---

[32] *Daily Advisor* (NY)
[33] *Commerical Advertiser* 24 October 1811.

Chapter 5

The case of the seizure of the schooner TWO BROTHERS took over 100 years to resolve in Congress as part of the French spoliation claims. The case was tried the 31st of October 1911 for the Columbian Insurance Co. of New York. The findings were as follows:

I. The schooner Two Brothers, whereof Isaac Lockwood was then master, sailed on a commercial voyage from Edenton, N.C. on or about May 27, 1800 bound to Trinidad. While peacefully pursuing said voyage she was seized on the high seas on 6th day of July, following, by the French privateer Bijou of Guadeloupe, . . . The prize crew took from the said Isaac Lockwood all his ships papers. August 13, 1800 the Two Brothers and cargo were condemned and ordered sold for the benefit of the captors by decree of the tribunal of commerce and prizes sitting at Guadeloupe. The grounds for condemnation were that the said schooner carried neither charter party, invoice, nor bill of lading as the captain confessed at his interrogation as to the other papers.
II. The Two Brothers was a duly registered vessel of the United States of 83 69/95 tons burthen, built in the State of New Jersey in the year 1799 an owned solely by John Bedient and Gideon Kimberly . . . and Walter Hubbell, a citizen of the United States residing in Windsor, N.C. After the condemnation aforesaid the former owners repossessed said vessel and reregistered her at New York October 28, 1800.
III. The cargo of the Two Brothers at the time of her capture consisted of lumber, fish and pork . . .
CONCLUSION OF LAW
The court decides as conclusions of law that said seizure and condemnation are not shown to have been illegal by satisfactory proof. . .[34]

In another case in the Connecticut Courts of 1886: a French Spoliation claim by Richard Hubbell Jr (370) was resolved by his grandchildren and great grandchildren. A total award of $553.42 was divided among ten descendants in 1909. Richard was lost at sea in 1811.

Vessels with Hubbell owners were often sailed under non-Hubbell masters. Rarely did a master also own the vessel and cargo. Hubbell masters often sailed ships owned by others, for example the Wetmore

---

[34] 63rd Congress, 3d Session HOUSE OF REPRESENTATIVES Document No. 1141.

Chapter 5

& Bros. vessels of Stratford, Connecticut: GOVERNOR, HULDAH, NANCY, PEGGY and the ship VICTORIA were all commanded by Hubbell's part of the time

An example of a Wetmore owned vessel was the sloop HULDAH, built in Stratford in 1784 and registered at Stratford from 1789 to 1794. She is described as 63 tons, length 56 feet 8 inches, draft 7 feet 2 inches, beam 18 feet 1 inch with one mast, and a square stern, Thaddeus Hubbell (488, 1768-1837) was her master.

Another Hubbell firm was Allen & Hubbell first noted in 1805 in New York and dissolved 5 May 1808[35]. It appears that Levi Hubbell (528, 1782-1872) married in 1802 the daughter of Nehemiah Allen and was made a partner in his father-in-law's business. The firm operated at the corner of Burling slip and South Street with cargoes of beef, coffee, Trinidad sugar, St Domingo coffee, black pepper, whale and sperm oil, and groceries. After the departure of Levi Hubbell, the firm continued as Nehemiah Allen & Son. Levi and family moved to New Orleans where his son, Henry Abraham Hubbell (1371, 1806-1829) died at the age of 23 on the ship AMERICA.

This period also saw the lost at sea Seaman Jabez Hubbell (532, 1770-1794) of Fairfield who died on the passage from the Turk Islands.[36] He had signed on under Captain Miller.

The sloop ARGO of Stratford was built in 1792 and registered at Stratford 1792-1793. She was 66 tons, length 58 feet 8 inches, draft, 7 feet, beam 19 feet 2 inches. She had one mast and a square stern. Her master was Wakeman Hubbell (496, 1762-1794). Wakeman was the son of Nathan Hubbell Jr (159) and Anna Wakeman. I have not found any newspaper references to voyages. However, Wakeman Hubbell brought the sloop JULIUS CAESAR home on 11 July 1795 with "67 hogsheads molasses, 3 tierces and 11 barrels for a total of

---

[35] *Mercantile Advertiser* (NY)
[36] *Connecticut Journal* 24 September 1794.

Chapter 5

7350 gallons; 28 barrels brown sugar (5520 lbs); 7 pots; 1 bag brown sugar (250 lbs); 5 small bags cotton & some loose cotton; 2 bags coffee (226 lbs) 375 lbs old iron; 1 barrel lime; 1 case gin; 11 straws of drinking glasses; 3 raw hides".[37] Also on board for ship use and not subject to customs was "4 gallons of rum in keg, 4 gallons claret wine, 2 bottles of gin, 10 lbs brown sugar and 15 lbs pot sugar"[38] This sloop at various times was also under the command of Ezekiel Hubbell (515, 1768-1834), William Hubbell (507, 1775-1805) and Thaddeus Hubbell.

The 66 ton sloop NABBY was built in Sag Harbor, New York in 1793 and enrolled 9 March 1795 in New York. She appears on a list of vessels in New York Harbor 28 November 1795.

The CAROLINE, a schooner owned by Ezekiel Hubbell was forced into the Cape by French cruisers in December 1794 and arrived in Boston the 23rd of the same month.

JULIA (2) was a sloop built in Fairfield 1801, registered in Fairfield and Stamford from 1801 to 1816 for the coastal trade. She was 27 tons, length 44 feet 6 inches, draft 4 feet 9 inches, beam 16 feet with one mast, and a square stern. Aaron Hubbell (535, 1778-1807) was master. He died of yellow fever at the age 29. He commanded the sloop JULIA of New York and Fairfield July 1805, owned by Walter Thorp. His daughter Elizabeth (1381) married Captain Jonathan Godfrey of the sloop ANNAWAN.

Usually all vessels carried both passengers and cargo since the easiest way to travel before railroads was still by water. Accommodations were primitive and the trip can be exciting and dangerous. In 1791 Uriah Bulkeley, ten years old, wrote about his trip from Connecticut to New York and return in a small sloop of 20 tons.

"We went to Mill River, now Southport and to New York in a small sloop, Walter Perry, master, his brother David hand, Job Perry, my father, myself and one

---

[37] Knapp p 120.
[38] Ibid.

Chapter 5

*female, passengers. The sloop only twenty tons, sails and vessel old, wind fresh at
N. E. When got to Norwalk Islands, it shut in so thick with snow that we hardly see
the length of the vessel, a heavy rolling sea and every soul on board deathly sick
except the female. Could hardly find anyone to steer, but we drifted along through
the Sound to Hart Island when it broke away, and went on to Riker's and anchored.
Beat down the next morning, and went into Burling Slip to head and our bowsprit
lay half-way across Pearl Street at the foot of John Street on the corner of which
was Rogers & Woolsey's hardware-store with a large gilt padlock for a sign which
was my guide back to the sloop as I lived on board. After about a week we started
for home wind S. E. In going through Hell Gate close hauled on the wind. There
was a large wood-sloop coming down before the wind with no one forward to look
out. We hail them, but could make no one could hear until close to us. She just
grazed our side and the bow- sprit caught in the after-leach of our mainsail and
unshipped our boom, broke the gaff in three places and took the whole sail off her
bow-sprit; took off our boat which was in tow. We made out as the tide was with us
to get up under our jib, against Riker's Island and anchored . . . Father and I went
ashore and slept. There was a tremendous gale that night.*
*Next day was pleasant. Mended and bent our sail and started for home. Arrived at
the dock at daylight next morning, walked home and commenced at Dr. Dwight's
Academy . . ."* [39]

As thousands of seamen passed through American ports, social
reformers recognized a need for seaman's benevolence. Seaman aid
societies were organized in all major ports. Targets for reform were
the dance halls and saloons designed to separate the sailor from his
money as soon as possible. Ministers were very active by distributing
Bibles and preaching on the streets about the evils of loose women
and drink. The government also recognized the need and Seaman's
Protective Certificates were issued:

NAME	AGE	BIRTH PLACE	DATE	NUMBER	DESCRIPTION	ME #
Ezra Hubbell	24	Weston MA	11 May 1809	42		1187
James Hubbell	21	Fairfield CT	29 Nov 1803	2704	5' 11" dark	540

---

[39] Partridge pp 75-76.

James Hubbell	18	Fairfield CT	17 March 1801	2067	5' 10"	540
William Hubbell	16	New London CT	16 July 1805	158		1731?
George S Hubbell	20	New Haven CT	28 Oct 1841	117		3934
Amon Hubbell	26	Danbury CT	29 June 1816	31		981

Table 1. From on-line data base at mysticseaport.com.

During this period Josiah Hubbell "died home at Old Mill, Capt. Josiah Hubbell, for many years employed in the coastal business from this port (Newfield ed.) to Boston".[40]

UNNAMED VESSELS (3)

Another set of trips without ship's name took place on the run between Connecticut and Boston from the end of 1753 until mid-1754. The vessel was a sloop and the master was Hubbell.

---

[40] *American Telegraphe* 4 November 1795.
[14] All Connecticut Wills and Probate Records 1609-1999 by Ancestry.

Chapter 6

The New Republic and a New Constitution
The Coastal Trade

Regulations for the coastal trade required that American vessels pay their tonnage duties yearly, all foreign vessels had to pay each time they entered port.

The PACKET (1) a sloop of Stratford was built in Stratford 1789. She was 32 tons, length 36 feet 2 inches, draft 5 feet 5 inches, beam 16 feet one mast and a square stern. She was enrolled 9 December 1789. Owners were Richard Hubbell (371, 1775-1811) of Fairfield and Asa Hubbell (361, 1757-1801) of Stratford. The master in 1795 was Richard Hubbell and in 1796 Asa Hubbell. April 1795 she made the Bridgeport to Philadelphia run, Master Richard Hubbell. In June 1795 under Asa Hubbell she commenced the Bridgeport to Philadelphia scheduled run. In 1796 she began a run from Bridgeport to New York. Customers could make the trip and were served meals on board.

"All persons indebted to us the subscribers for PASSAGE & BOARD (only) to and from New York, are hereby requested to make immediate payment or their accounts will be put in suit without discrimination ASA HUBBELL, JOHN BROOKS". [41]

Captain Asa Hubbell of Bridgeport fell overboard in the North River near West Point and drowned 16 July 1801.[42]

The schooner DOLPHIN was built in 1792 at Fairfield, and her home ports were Fairfield and Stonington. She was 23 tons, length 41 feet, draft 4 feet 9 inches beam 16 feet inches and registered at Fairfield from 1796 to 1800 and from 1802 to 1815. She was registered at one time for cod fishing. Aaron Hubbell (535) was the master when she arrived in New York from Fairfield 4 September 1799 with a cargo of muslins and oats.

The schooner REBECCA & POLLY arrived in New York 21 May 1799 with a load of coal from Norfolk after a 5 day voyage.

---

[41] *American Telegraphe* 20 April 1796.
[42] Balance 16 July 1801.

"New York Coal Company,
Are landing a cargo of Virginia coal, of the first quality, from on board the
schooner Rebecca and Polly, Capt Hubble, laying at the Coffee-house slip, which
will be sold low, if immediate application is made to the captain on board. Mr. P
McGuire, no 45 Nassau street, no 222 Pearl street or no 60 Naden? Lane.
N. B. The above schooner will be ready to take in freight immediately for Norfolk,
Petersburg and Richmond. Apply as above."

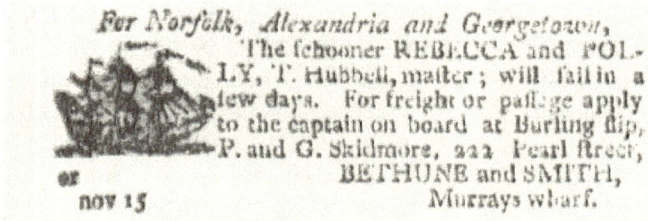

Figure 10. *Daily Advertiser* 20 Nov 1799. Early American Newspapers op.cit.

The coaster HERO cleared New York for Boston 12 June 1804 and
arrived 9 July.

The first HOPE (1) was a sloop of Newfield CT built in 1793. She
was 86 tons, length 63 feet 3 inches, beam 20 feet 7 inches, draft 7
feet 10 inches with one deck, one mast and a square stern. Salmon
Hubbell was master 6 September 1794.

The schooner BETSY/BETSEY advertised for freight or passengers
to Norfolk and Alexandria, Virginia after she arrived in New York
from Snow Hill, Maryland 18 August 1801.

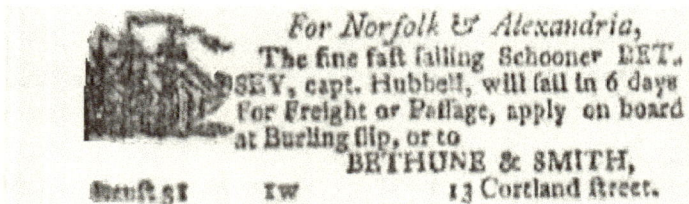

Figure 11. *Daily Advertiser* 3 September 1801, Early American Newspapers op. cit.

The sloop JEFFERSON was built at Fairfield in 1801 and registered
from 1802 to 1813 at Fairfield. The JEFFERSON was 32 tons, length

44 feet 6 inches, beam 16 feet 3 inches, draft 5 feet 5 inches. She was registered for the coasting trade, Aaron Hubbell (534) master. She arrived in Newport, Rhode Island from Fairfield on 9 April 1802 and in New York from Boston 23 July 1803.

The coaster SALLY & MARY was in port New York 21 to 28 August 1802 recently arrived from Snow Hill.

The sloop RACHEL arrived in New York from Philadelphia 9 May 1795.

Little is known of the sloop CUMSTOCK. She cleared New York for Providence, Rhode Island 1 August 1805 under the command of Ezekiel Hubbell (514).

The FACTOR of Stratford was a sloop (sometimes listed as a coaster) built in 1797 at Stratford and registered 1797-1803. She is described as 70 tons, length 55 feet, draft 6 feet 5 inches, beam 17 feet 9 inches, with 1 mast. and a square stern, capacity 600 barrels. Ezra Hubbell (365, 1769-1804) was master in 1797. In a New York ad of 27 December 1803 she was scheduled to sail in the 30th for Boston. She arrived in Boston on the 21 January 1803 and sailed for Washington, North Carolina, arriving there in 8 days. She returned to New York. January 29, 1803 she sailed from Salem to New York and in February to Boston and back to New York. She took another trip to Washington in May, then off to St Bartholomew in July, finally arriving in New York in August.

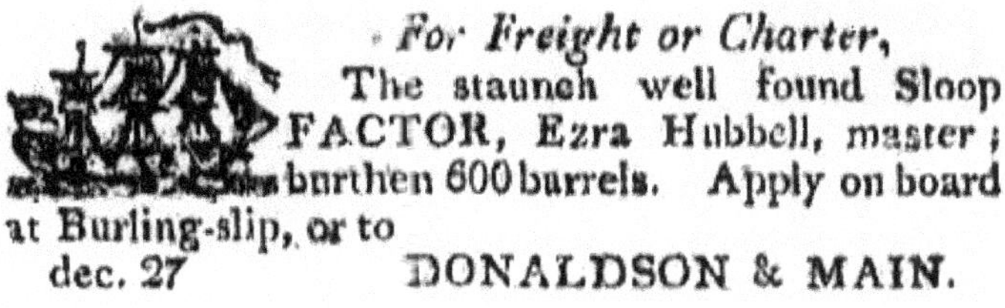

> For Freight or Charter,
> The staunch well found Sloop
> FACTOR, Ezra Hubbell, master;
> burthen 600 barrels. Apply on board
> at Burling-slip, or to
> dec. 27   DONALDSON & MAIN.

Figure 12. *Commercial Advertiser* 1 July 1802, Early American Newspapers op.cit.

Chapter 6

The HARMONY, a sloop built in Stratford 1800 was registered in Derby 1801-1805. She is described as 40 tons, length 51 feet 7 inches, draft 5 feet 7 inches, beam 16 feet 7 inches with 1 mast. William Hubbell (506, 1775-1805) is listed as master. The HARMONY cleared New York on 10 February 1804 described as a coaster and proceeded to Vienna, Maryland and Richmond before returning to Boston on 21 June.

The coaster ELIZA (first with that name), 66 tons was probably built at Oyster Bay, New York in 1802 and registered 10 September 1802. She made two runs from Hudson to New York in August and September 1802.

The sloop NANCY was built during 1796 at New Haven and registered at Stratford from 1800 to 1803. She is described as 85 tons, length 62 feet 2 inches, draft 8 feet 6 inches, beam 18 feet 8 inches with 2 masts and a square stern. Her master in 1796 was William Hubbell (506). She arrived in Boston from the Hudson 24 July 1804. She was next reported arriving in Charleston 23 April 1805, 9 days out of New York. She arrived in New York 15 May 1805 from Savannah. Other voyages were recorded among these ports ending at Charleston on 6 December 1805 when she arrived with a cargo of oats, beef and hay.

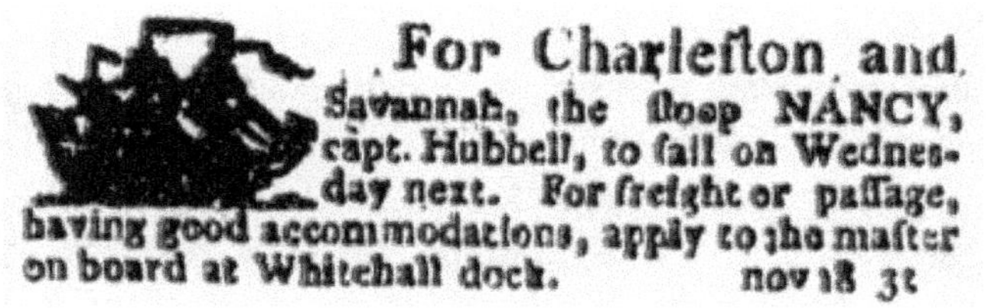

For Charleston and Savannah, the sloop NANCY, capt. Hubbell, to sail on Wednesday next. For freight or passage, having good accommodations, apply to the master on board at Whitehall dock. nov 18 3t

Figure 13. *New York Gazette* 28 Nov 1805, Early American Newspapers op. cit.

The schooner POLLY (1), like many of the vessels engaged in both coastal and West Indies trade. She made two trips between Philadelphia and Newbern, North Carolina in June 1790. July 1, 1790

29

Chapter 6

she cleared Newbern for the West Indies, and in October she arrived in Newbern from Philadelphia. October 1804 she arrived in Philadelphia with a load of cotton from New Orleans.

The schooner WEALTHY cleared Philadelphia for Charleston 11 December 1804. In January 1805 she put into Bermuda in distress, being blown off course, finally arriving in Charleston 16 April. She returned to Philadelphia 6 May 1805.

"The schooner Wealthy, Hubbell, from Philadelphia for Charleston, after suffering almost every calamity incident to life of a mariner, put into St Georges Bermuda in distress, having been blown off the coast seven times. A letter from Capt Hubbell mentions that he arrived in Bermuda on the 26 of January and that five vessels arrived there in distress since he did, bound on the coast. Capt Hubbell mentions that he was generously supplied and handsomely treated by the commander of the British frigate Tartar, who arrived at Bermuda 2 days after the Wealthy. . ."[43]

The sloop ACKERLY cleared Baltimore 17 June 1806 for New York, arriving after a 4 day trip. She sailed from New York to Boston 8 July 1806. Mr. S. Ackerly operated a ship yard in New York c1790.

For Kingfton, Jamaica,
(To fail in a few days)
The BRIG
LAVINIA,
Samuel Hubbell, mafter.
For freight only, apply to
Philips, Cramond & Co.
Dec. 6
d:t

Figure 14. *Gazette of the United States* 6 Dec 1794, Early American Newspapers, op. cit.

In 1795 he advertised a pilot boat for sale.

---

[43] *New York Gazette* 1 March 1805.

Chapter 6

To be Sold,

A faft failing
PILOT BOAT,
Only about 4 years old, well found,
with new fails, cables, rigging, &c.—
may be put in bufinefs at a very fmall
expence, being lately well repaired, now lying at John
M'Culloch's wharf. For terms apply to
Capt. SAMUEL HUBBLE,
Dec. 5 .tuth s,3t, No. 16, Queen ftreet.

Figure 15. *Philadelphia Gazette* 8 December 1795, Early American Newspapers, op. cit.

TWO BROTHERS, a schooner of New Brunswick, from and for Charleston, engaged in trade along the coast, overseas to Europe and in the West Indies. She was built in New Jersey 1799, 83 tons Burthen owned by John Bedient, Gideon Kimberly of New York and Walter Hubbell of Windsor, North Carolina. She was reported condemned at Guadeloupe 13 August 1800 along with her cargo of lumber fish and pork. The grounds for condemnation were that she was carrying goods not on the bill of lading. She (or another with same name) was cleared New York 3 December 1806 for Charleston arriving on 22 December. She cleared Charleston 10 January 1807 for Maderia, Spain and returned 28 February with a cargo of wine. She cleared Wilmington 9 June 1807 for Jamaica arriving 29 June 1807. She next appears in Havana 18 October 1807 under command of Captain Lavington "formerly Hubble". October 17, 1810 she appears again under Hubbell command clearing New London for Antigua.

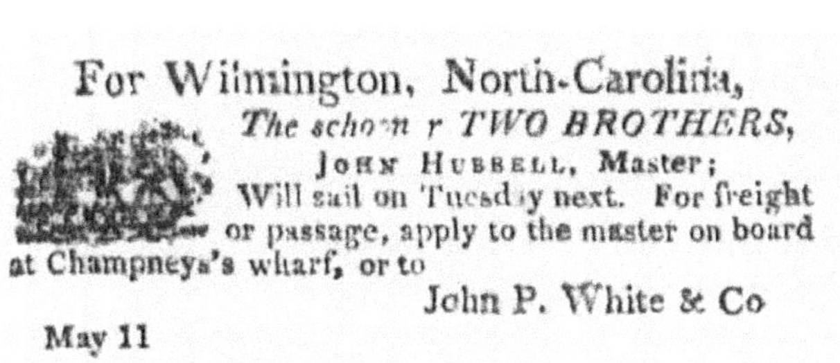

For Wilmington, North-Carolina,

The schoo'n r *TWO BROTHERS,*
JOHN HUBBELL, Master;
Will sail on Tuesd'y next. For freight
or passage, apply to the master on board
at Champneys's wharf, or to
John P. White & Co
May 11

Figure 16. *City Gazette* 12 May 1807, Early American Newspapers op. cit.

31

Chapter 6

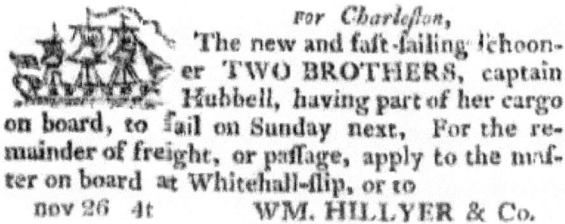

Figure 17. *New York Gazette* 26 Nov 1806, Early American Newspapers op. cit.

The schooner ELIZABETH (1) arrived in New York from North Carolina 6 March 1798 and returned to Edenton, North Carolina on 26 March 1798

The sloop ELIZABETH (2) of Amboy floundered at 18.39 N 69.30 16 April 1809, the crew of 6 men became exhausted working the pumps and the cargo and crew were removed.

"Captain Hubbell of the sloop Elizabeth, returns his sincere thanks to Captain William Miller of the brig Lovely Lass for his humanity in relieving himself, supercargo and crew after taking them up at sea, and removing them from his foundered vessel, and his general attention during the passage to Philadelphia 26 April".[44]

The sloop CATY-MARIA was recorded in one voyage under command of Captain M. Hubbell from Norfolk to New York in July 1805. She was probably build in Norwich, Connecticut and enrolled 26 October 1802.

The schooner GEORGE (2) made the New York to Washington, North Carolina trip at least 10 times from November 1809 to August 1810 with cargoes of cotton and Naval stores.

The schooner GOOD INTENT of 22 tons was built at Branford, Connecticut and enrolled 11 September 1793. She cleared New York on 29 April 1795 bound for New Brunswick.

---

[44] *Poulson's American Daily Advertiser* 26 April 1809.

UNNAMED VESSELS (4)

A large number of round trips between Boston and ports in Connecticut were reported from 5 Aug 1758 to 5 Aug 1761. The name of the vessel is unknown as well as type of vessel. Usually the trip was reported outward on the first day, at sea one day and entered in on the third day. No cargo was reported. The master's name was Hubbell.

Chapter 7

The New Republic and a New Constitution
China and European Trade

Before American Independence, the British trade with China was a monopoly of the East Indian Company and Americans were not allowed to trade with China. Now independent, the merchants of the new country eagerly looked for opportunities to trade with the Far East. The first vessel to sail around the Cape of Good Hope to China was the EMPRESS OF CHINA in 1785. Soon our Hubbell Captains took to overseas voyages in increasing numbers.

The brig LIVINA/LAVINA master Samuel Hubbell cleared Philadelphia 23 June 1794 for Cadiz. She left Malaga on 1 October 1794 and arrived in Philadelphia 20 November 1794 with a cargo of Malaga wine in hogheads and quarter casks, sun raisins in barrels, muscatel raisins in boxes and jars, figs in barrels, shelled almonds in boxes, lemons and grapes in jars.

The brigantine AMELIA (1), 106 tons, was probably built in Connecticut 1785 and was registered 2 February 1790. Departing London and after a voyage of 56 days she arrived in Baltimore via New York 26 May 1796. During this trip she was stopped by a privateer brig of 6 guns (see below). She is next reported in Bordeaux, France August 1795 under the command of Captain E. Hubbell. She arrived in New York May 1796 after being stopped again by a privateer.

"The following is communicated Capt. Hubbell, of the Brig AMELIA, who arrived here last Sunday in 37 days from London: On my passage out of the mouth of the channel, fell in with a privateer brig of 6 guns; the captain sent his boat, and ordered me on board; after going there, he desired me to go down to his cabin, where he examined my papers, and told me he was a Frenchman, and I was a legal prize to him, and forbid me to go on deck. I desired him to produce his papers, which he refused; and while I was disputing with him about the impropriety of his conduct, another sail hove in sight, which stood for us; he immediately gave up my papers, and sent me on board my own vessel, but plundered me of my spy-glass, and several other articles. I was likewise boarded from the ship, but they treated me very politely. The ship was from Brest, carried 18 guns, and they informed me they had sent in five valuable prizes in 8 days. He also says, there were a great

Chapter 7

many cruzers (sic) fitting out at Brest and other ports of France, who took a great many vessels from the English, which they fitted out immediately. Nothing more worth notice. E. HUBBELL- Brig AMELIA" [45]

Captain Ezekiel Hubbell in the ship CITIZEN was heavily engaged in trade with the West Indies (See Chapter 8) but made several trips overseas. The story is told in Walter Hubbell's *History of the Hubbell Family* but is worth retelling here. Ezekiel was a clerk on board vessels owned by Richard and Amos Hubbell at the age of fourteen. He was successful as a master and supercargo and in he purchased the ship ENTERPRISE of 250 tons to fulfill a plan to trade with the wealth of Spain on the Pacific coast of South America. She cleared New York 28 January 1800 under command of Ezekiel Hubbell with a crew of thirty. He made slow progress crossing the equator and since the ship was not coppered, she put into an inlet about 45 degrees south where the crew careened the vessel on the beach and cleaned her bottom of barnacles and sea grass. She was reported at 46 South on 10 May 1800. They had a stormy time passing Cape Horn in early February, reached the Pacific and put into Valparaiso, Chili. At this time, the crew was suffering from scurvy and the governor granted permission to remain in port for a reasonable time. Since no vessels except Spanish were allowed to trade in the port, the ENTERPRISE and crew were closely watched. Ezekiel obtained permission to visit the capital, Santiago de Chili and called upon General O'Higgins and asked to sell his cargo which was refused. After ten days, he achieved a conditional sale of the majority of his cargo at Conception, 300 miles south of Valparaiso. An agent was placed on board and they sailed to the beautiful bay with snow covered mountains in the distance. When the ENTERPRISE arrived a boat was sent ashore but was surprised by an ambush. The boat and party were retrieved and Ezekiel left at once. He sailed to the North West coast of American and put into the port at San Blas, New Spain (Mexico) but was fired upon by the forts guarding the harbor and departed. He apparently put in to San Diego for wood and water when she was described as 10 guns and 21 men owned by Hay & Thorn. He proceeded on to Nootka Sound and then to China, calling

[45] *Greenleaf's New York Journal* 17 May 1796.

Chapter 7

at the Sandwich Islands (Hawaii) and the Russian settlements near Kamchatka. She arrived in Manila 8 July 1800 and then Canton after a voyage of 150 days. In *Boston Men on the Northwest Coast*, Mary Mallory says the ENTERPRISE was engaged in illegal trade on the California Coast. Ms. Mallory states that ENTERPRISE left New York February 1800 and was reported by Russian sources at Kodiak in November to January 1802 and then on to Canton. ENTERPRISE arrived in Bridgeport 26 June 1802 after a voyage of 29 months, and 140 days from Canton. Her cargo consisted of Hyson, Young Hyson, Hyson Shulon and Souchong teas, silks, nankeens, sinchews, Taffetys, satins, sewing silks, umbrellas and lying at Crane Wharf.

"Ship Enterprize, Capt Hubbell, which sailed from this port in company with the Pagasus and long since a missing ship, we are happy to learn, was safe arrived at her port of destination in the Pacific Ocean on the 8th of July 1800 and it is expected she has proceeded on her voyage to Canton".[46]

"Bridgeport, (Con.) June 30. On Thursday last arrived off this port, on her way to New York the ship Enterprize, Ezekiel Hubbell of this place, Master, in 140 days from Canton – Capt. Hubbell has performed a circuitous and lengthy voyage of nearly two years and a half since he left New York, and we expect has met with success proportionate to the greatness of the undertaking. Capt. H. lost his 2d mate and two others of his crew.

Capt. Hubbell's rout(e) has been, round Cape Horn up the Pacific Ocean, upon the Northwest coast, and thence to Canton – in the course of which has had many scenes of danger, of anxiety, and some profitable traffic: one of the natives of Sandwich Islands (where Cook was killed) he brought home with him who is now in this place at school; a likely and ingenious lad of about twelve years of age, of an olive complexion, black straight hair, &c – who understands much, and begins to speak our language. . ."[47]

The arrangements made for Ezekiel Hubbell's first voyage to China consisted of 3 equal shares between Isaac Moses & Son, Hoyt & Tom and Ezekiel Hubbell. Great latitude was given to the Master and Supercargo concerning the conduct of the business. *The Daily Sitka Sentinel* of 11 December 1997 reported that the ENTERPRISE called at Kodiak and probably traded with Russian settlers and natives at

---

[46] *Philadelphia Gazette* 24 Sept 1801.
[47] *Commercial Advertiser* 1 July 1802.

Chapter 7

Old Sitka. The same paper in 16 June 2006 said that the ENTERPRISE of 240 tons left New York February 1799 under Captain Ezekiel Hubbell and was a pioneer in the illegal trade on the California coast.

In the spring of 1803 Ezekiel Hubbell purchased a share of the 200 ton brig CATHERINE RAY was one of six ships Ezekiel Hubbell sailed to the Orient. She left New York 12 May 1803, sailed for 100 days to Canton, China and returned 19 April 1804 after 136 days at sea.

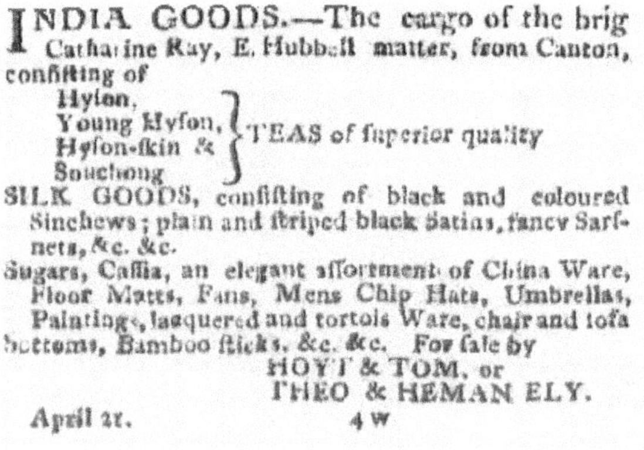

INDIA GOODS.—The cargo of the brig
Catharine Ray, E. Hubbell master, from Canton,
consisting of
   Hyson,
   Young Hyson, } TEAS of superior quality
   Hyson-skin &
   Souchong
SILK GOODS, consisting of black and coloured
   Sinchews; plain and striped black Satins, fancy Sarf-
   nets, &c. &c.
Sugars, Cassia, an elegant assortment of China Ware,
   Floor Matts, Fans, Mens Chip Hats, Umbrellas,
   Paintings, lacquered and tortois Ware, chair and sofa
   bottoms, Bamboo sticks. &c. &c.   For sale by
               HOYT & TOM, or
               THEO & HEMAN ELY.
April 21.   4 W

Figure 18. *Daily Advertiser* 21 April 1804

He made a second voyage in the CATHERINE RAY returning home in the spring of 1805 when the brig was sold. As recently as 2011 a relic of Ezekiel's voyages surfaced. A Rhinoceros horn from 19th century China that once belonged to Ezekiel was offered at auction. It was described as a reticulated Rhinoceros horn libation cup with the eight immortals and rocky ledges, trees, clouds, a dragon, tiger and goats on a black openwork base. It was valued from $60,000 to $80,000 dollars.

In June 1804, Captain Hubbell in the ship CITIZEN cleared New York for Amsterdam She returned with a cargo of Amsterdam gin and arrived in New York in October.

Chapter 7

"For Amsterdam, the well known ship Citizen, E. Hubbell, master, newly coppered and well found, will be . . . without delay; now ready to receive a cargo, considerable part of which is engaged . . . [48]

She cleared New York for Amsterdam 7 March 1805 under an arrangement with Hoyt & Tom and was sighted at the Isle of Wight 32 days out of New York. She arrived in Amsterdam in June and then made the 124 day journey to Canton. She was at the Whampoa anchorage in December and returned to New York 13 May 1806. Her cargo consisted of gunpowder, lacquered ware, floor mats, tea, china ware, nankeens, china root, silks, cassin and alum.

The ship AUGUSTUS cleared New York for Amsterdam 17 February 1807 under the command of Ezekiel Hubbell. She was built in 1805 at Norwich, Connecticut, drew 283 tons and was registered 15 March 1806. The AUGUSTUS was owned in equal shares by Moses & Son, Hoyt & Tom, and Ezekiel Hubbell. She was in port Amsterdam June 1807 and arrived at the Isle de France September 1807 where he purchased a cargo of cotton. He delivered the cotton to China and returned with tea for which he left a note.

"$103,000   *CANTON, CHINA,*
January 15th 1808
Twelve months after date, for value received, I promise to pay to the order of Houqua, Hong merchant, one hundred and three thousand dollars for cargo of tea per Ship AUGUSTUS with and interest at 12 Per cent per Annum.
                             Ezekiel Hubbell" [49]

She sailed from Canton October 1807 and was sighted at the Cape of Good Hope June 1808. She was intercepted by a British cruiser 2 July 1808 was sent to Plymouth, England and released in August of that same year. The cargo of tea was designed for the market in Holland, but when the AUGUSTUS reached the British Isles, ports in Holland were under blockade. According to Ezekiel, he slipped the blockade and off loaded his cargo of tea in Amsterdam and

---

[48] *New York Gazette* 16 February 1805.

[49] *History of the Hubbell Family*, p75.

eventually paid the note to Houqua with interest. Ezekiel was semi-retired until after the War of 1812. His later voyages are covered in Chapter 9.

The ship OCEAN arrived in New York 10 November 1801 from Liverpool. Nothing further was found regarding this voyage, the trip, or Captain Hubbell.

The ship JANE of New Orleans was 198 tons length 81 feet 6 inches, beam 24 feet 9 inches, draft 11 feet 5 inches, she had 3 masts, a square stern, a woman figurehead, and a round tuck. The master was Ephraim Hubbell. The JANE was noted in port Lisbon from September to December 1806 to sail for Antwerp in 6 days. She was in port Bordeaux on 28 May 1807 and lost at sea when sailing for Amsterdam on 1 October 1807. The crew was saved.

A single entry for the ship CAMILA, she cleared New York for Liverpool 7 April 1803.

The JOHN & MARY sailed from Wilmington, North Carolina for Liverpool 14 May 1801.

Ezekiel Hubbell was the owner and master of the ELIZA ANN. She arrived in New York from Cadiz 5 June 1809 and Ezekiel sought legislative relief for paid fees.

GEORGE, (1) a brig out of Philadelphia cleared Philadelphia for Spain 25 June 1791 and she arrived in New York 9 October 1791 with a cargo of dry goods. She then made a quick trip to St Martins and Bilboa arriving back to Philadelphia in October and a similar trip ending in early 1792. She cleared Philadelphia in May 1792 for a trip to France, retuning to Philadelphia 14 September 1792.

Chapter 8

The New Republic and a New Constitution
The West Indies

As a result of the American Revolution, trade to the British Islands was restricted but trade to the other islands increased. By 1790 total trade with the West Indies was greater than before the Revolution.[50] The "Long" embargo of 22 December 1801 provided that all American vessels were prohibited from leaving for foreign ports and no foreign vessels could take cargoes out. It was repealed 1 March 1809.

The brig JUNIUS BRUTUS arrived in Newfield from Boston 14 November 1787. She is next noted in New York from Fairfield 23 May 1791. She made at least 2 trips to the West Indies and was at sea in 1792. February 1793 JUNIUS BRUTUS owned by Richard and Amos Hubbell headed for Martinique with 99 bushels and 113 half bushels of salt beef and 7 bushels of pork.[51]

Wilson Hubbell (374, 1773-1796), owner and master of the brig AURORA put her up for sale May 1795. She had recently returned from a voyage from Philadelphia to Cape Francois and return.

The snow/brig KATY (CATY) left Bridgeport 30 October 1795 and was wrecked on her maiden voyage. She was built in Newfield shipyard September 1795 and was registered 26 October 1795, owner merchant Amos Hubbell, Ezekiel and Wilson Hubbell mariners. She was wrecked at sea at Anguilla, the cargo and rigging were saved. Captain Wilson Hubbell was in command.

---

[50] Labaree p. 171.
[51] Knapp p. 120.

FOR SALE.

THE Brigantine *AURORA*, Wilfon Hubbell, Mafter : burthen about 2000 barrels Well built and can be fitted for fea at a fmall expence—if not fold in ten days, fhe will then be for *FREIGHT* or *CHARTER* To any port in Europe. For terms apply to
P. WETMORE & BROTHERS.
No. 85 Wall-ftreet.
Who will on Monday land from on board of faid Brig,
12 tons Old Lead,
10 do. Old Iron, and
1 do. Old Brafs. =
April 25.   tf.

Figure 19. *American Minerva*, 4 May 1795. Early American Newspapers op. cit.

The sloop ENDEAVOR was built at Stratford in 1794 and registered in Newfield 1794-1796. She is described as 74 tons, length 60 feet 8 inches, draft 7 feet 5 inches, beam 19 feet 4 inches 1 mast, and a square stern. Josiah Hubbell and Wilson Hubbell were masters. Josiah Hubbell sailed her from Boston to Bridgeport to New York and Newfield in 1795. Wilson Hubbell sailed her to the West Indies in 1796. In December 1796, the sloop ENDEAVOR, Wilson Hubbell of Newfield was taken by the French and carried into Guadalupe for adjudication.

"By letter Capt Wilson Hubbel of sloop Endeavor we learn that his vessel and cargo has been cleared; and that he is now at liberty to sell his cargo, part of which he has already disposed of to the French government".[52]

The ship SALLY & BETSEY was 117 tons built in Newfield, Connecticut 1793 registered 15 February 1796. The SALLY & BETSEY was originally owned by the Wetmores but was condemned

---

[52] *American Telegraphe* 14 December 1796.

in New York and to be auctioned off. Ezekiel won the bid for $1,750.[53] Her master was Wilson Hubbell 6 February 1797 and the owner Ezekiel Hubbell 1797. She made frequent trips to the West Indies in 1796 and 1797 under Ezekiel Hubbell. January 1797 she touched at the harbor's mouth at Newfield bound to New York. A number of vessels bound for New York were frozen in the port. November 1797 she was chased by a French privateer. She appears on the condemned List of Spoliations by France.

One voyage of the brig FLY is recorded when she cleared Philadelphia for Petit Guave 14 February 1797.

The DELIGHT, a sloop built in 1794 Weatherfield, Connecticut and registered in Newfield 1794-95 and from 1779-98. She was described as 60 tons, length 55 feet, draft 7 feet, beam 18 feet 3 inches with a square stern. The DELIGHT was owned by Ezra Hubbell and Ezra Hubbell was master in 1794 as well as Wilson Hubbell.

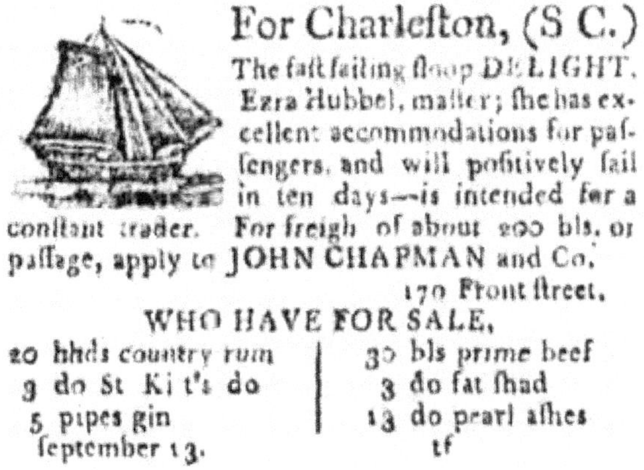

For Charlefton, (S C.)
The faft failing floop DELIGHT, Ezra Hubbel, mafter; fhe has excellent accommodations for paffengers, and will pofitively fail in ten days—is intended for a conftant trader. For freigh of about 200 bls. or paffage, apply to JOHN CHAPMAN and Co.
170 Front ftreet.
WHO HAVE FOR SALE,
20 hhds country rum | 30 bls prime beef
9 do St Ki t's do | 3 do fat fhad
5 pipes gin | 13 do pearl afhes
feptember 13. | tf

Figure 20. *Minerva* 22 Sept 1797. Early American Newspapers op. cit.

The DELIGHT cleared New York on 1 October 1797 and arrived in Savanna by way of Charleston and St Thomas on 3 November 1797 with a box of muslins for Kennedy & Parker. She cleared Savanna

---

[53] Knapp p. 125.

Chapter 8

28 Nov 1797. She was under the command of Wilson Hubbell in March 1799 when she was reported in New Providence and Havana. It was during this voyage that she was captured by a French privateer. The Captain of the privateer placed his first mate in command of the DELIGHT, with two French seamen. The French captain took two of Captain Hubbell's men and sailed away. The third day after the capture, the French mate ordered Captain Hubbell's mate to take the helm and leaving Captain Hubbell guarded by the French seamen, went to sleep. Wilson eluded the guards, entered the cabin and took possession of his sword and pistols. He overpowered the two guards retook command and turned for home. Later he released the French mate and ate supper with him. After dinner, they walked the deck together and Wilson offered the Frenchman a segar (cigar). The Frenchman dropped the segar at Wilson's feet, grabbed his ankles and threw him overboard.[54]

The sloop KINGSTON arrived in Philadelphia 1 July 1756 from Jamaica, Eleazer Hubbel, master.

The schooner MANHATTAN, William Hubbell master sank suddenly and the master and crew spent 2 days in a boat and arrived at New Providence 17 November 1802.

The brig PROVIDENCE arrived at Nassau from Newfield 13 June 1800.

The schooner INDUSTRY (2) arrived in New York from Guadalope 4 October 1793. She is again mentioned 13 October 1804 when cleared for Charleston from Philadelphia. She returned to port on 25 October leaky.

The schooner HAZARD sailed from St Kitts on 1 July 1797 and arrived in Edenton, North Carolina 13 days later. She was condemned at Guadalupe in December 1797.

---

[54] *History of the Hubbell Family* by Walter Hubbell, 1881 p.81.

Chapter 8

The ship MARY (1) operated from Charleston to St Domingo in 1805. March 1806 she declared for New York.

The only recorded voyage of the sloop GOVERNOR occurred in 1795 when she arrived in Antigua from Newfield on 31 March. She then sailed under the command of Ezra Hubbell on 2 April 1795, arriving in Bridgeport on 22 April.

The schooner HARRICT arrived in New York 16 October 1807 after a 14 day trip from Washington, North Carolina. She cleared on 28 October 1807 for the Turks Islands and arrived in December at Washington. The next record under Hubble command occurs on 11 February 1819 when she arrives at Holme's Hole.

The VOLUSIA, a sloop, was 82 tons and built 1802 at Stratford Connecticut, registered 7 Dec 1820 in New York, her master was Thaddeus Hubbell (488. 1768-1837) on 12 August 1811 owned by Stephen Burroughs Jr. and Daniel Lewis. She was active from September to November 1811 between Bridgeport and St Barts. October 22 1811 Thaddeus Hubbell arrived from St Barts with a cargo for himself.[55]

The ship FRIENDSHIP was possibly built at Berwick, Maine, registered in New York 1791 and was 183 tons. Commanded by Samuel Hubbell, she cleared Philadelphia 28 November 1792 and arrived at Alexandria in December. She was reported at Falmouth in April 1793 and was captured by the Kings ships when homeward bound from Nantz. According to the British, she had French property onboard and flying the French National colors when taken by the privateer ALEXANDER, Captain Shaw of Antigua. The FRIENDSHIP appears on a list of ships captured and brought into the port of Kingston, Jamaica. After all French property was confiscated, and a trial by the Court of the Admiralty, she was released and arrived in Philadelphia 9 September 1793.

---

[55] Knapp p. 121.

Chapter 8

The LORD JOHN was a sloop registered in 1791 in Stratford with the following description: 45 tons, length 47 feet, draft 5 feet 6 inches, beam 16 feet and a square stern. Ezekiel Hubbell was master in 1791. The LORD JOHN arrived in New York from St Thomas 27 June 1791 and sailed again for St Thomas and return. She cleared for Norfolk from New York 20 August 1791 and cleared for Stratford September 1791.

A single entry was found for the schooner BROTHERS, she arrived in Baltimore from Antigua 3 August 1796, Captain Hubble.

The schooner NANCY & MARY was one of the few vessels with a Hubbell captain out of Baltimore. She was reported arriving at Norfolk from Antigua in May 1806 and again in June. She cleared Baltimore for Antigua in August and returned to Baltimore in November. She arrived in Baltimore on 4 June 1807 from Guadalupe.

JOHN & ELCY, a schooner was in port Kingston from Baltimore 18 August 1804.

The only recorded voyage of the sloop GOVERNOR, under Hubbell command occurred in 1795 when she arrived in Antigua from Newfield on 31 March. She then sailed under the command of Ezra Hubbell on 2 April 1795, arriving in Bridgeport on 22 April.

Probably originally owned by Wetmore Brothers then sold to Mathias Nicoll 1795, the 106 ton brig JULIUS CAESAR (2) arrived in Bridgeport from Frenchman's Bay 24 August 1796, master Thaddeus Hubbell. Amos Hubbell's brig JULIUS CAESAR went down in 1799 on her way home from West Indies, crew escaped in a long boat but the Captain Abel Wakelee drowned.[56].

The ship VICTORIA 173 tons was built 1794 Stratford, Connecticut and registered 8 February 1796. She sailed to the West Indies out of New York in 1794 to 1795 and again 1805. June 22, 1795 she arrived

---

[56] Knapp p 111.

Chapter 8

in New York minus her mizzenmast lost in a gale of wind in the Gulf Stream. Her cargo was usually Jamaican sugar.

The brig TRITON, Samuel Hubbell, master sailed from Philadelphia to Alexandria and return in September 1795. She was scheduled to depart for Cape Francois 17 November 1795.

For *Alexandria,*
The brig TRITON,
Samuel Hubbell, Master ;
A good staunch vessel, with excel-
lent accommodations for passengers—will sail on
Thursday next. For freight or passage apply to the
captain on board at Clifford's wharf, or to
JOSEPH MUSSI,
Sept. 5   No. 37, north Water street.

Figure 21. *Philadelphia Gazette* 8 Sept 1795. Early American Newspapers op. cit.

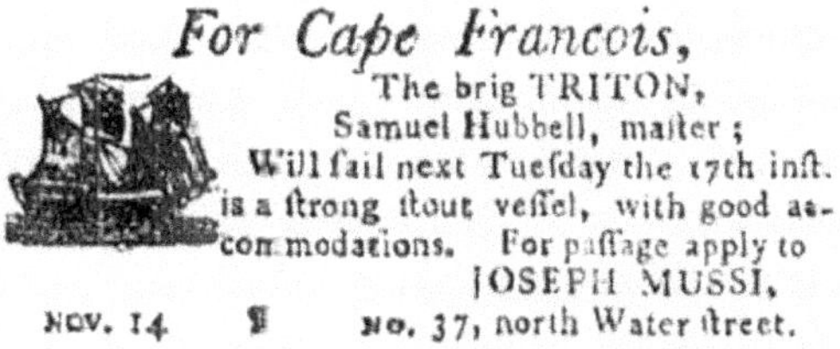

For *Cape Francois,*
The brig TRITON,
Samuel Hubbell, master ;
Will sail next Tuesday the 17th inst.
is a strong stout vessel, with good ac-
commodations. For passage apply to
JOSEPH MUSSI,
NOV. 14   No. 37, north Water street.

Figure 22. *Philadelphia Gazette* 21 Nov 1795, Early American Newspapers op. cit.

Ship CITIZEN 282 tons, was built in 1791 in Philadelphia and registered 18 October 1797. Under the command of Captain Ezekiel Hubbell, she made trips to Havana in February and April 1798.

"For Havannah, the ship Citizen, Ezekiel Hubbel master, will mount twelve or Fourteen carriage guns of 4,6 and 12 pounders and is intended to have from 35 to 40 men, will be ready to take in on Monday next, and will be dispatched with all convenient speed. For Freight apply to Monson Hayt, No 142 Water Street or to HOYT and TOM, Crane wharf"[57]

"THE SHIP CITIZEN, Mounting 14 guns, and carrying 40 men, will sail for the Havanna on the 28th inst, will take a few vessels under her convoy, on moderate

---

[57] *Daily Advertiser* 4 August 1798.

Chapter 8

terms. Apply to Capt. Hubbell on board – to Monson Hayt, 142 Water Street, or HOYT & TOM, Crane wharf."[58]

In 1798 Ezekiel Hubbell's ship CITIZEN was taken into Halifax by an English cruiser.

She cleared New York on 31 August 1798 bound for Havana and the armed ship CITIZEN, Captain Hubbell of 18 guns 29 days from the Havanah came out with 16 American vessels under convoy. Late that same year she sailed for Martinique and St Thomas.

"For Martinique and St. Thomas, the well known ship CITIZEN, Ezekiel Hubbell, master, mounting 16 Carriage guns and intended to carry 40 men, will be dispatched with all convenient speed – For freignt or passage, having good accommodations, apply to the master on board, or to HOYT & TOM Crane wharf. [59]

Scurvy was the plague of the sea. Mariners died by the tens of thousands and the presence of other diseases, dietary deficiencies and a damp ship at sea for months made diagnosis very difficult. Although not usually a problem for short voyages, scurvy was always a threat. After centuries of false cures, political interference and indifference, Gilbert Blain, attached to Admiral Sir George Rodney's West Indies fleet finally documented the cure in 1783.[60] That Ezekiel Hubbell recognized the importance of citrus is apparent in a spring 1799 announcement which stated that "12 kegs of lime juice, ship Citizen, Hubble, Havana in the Public store, if not claimed in ten days will be sold as the law directs". In March, the CITIZEN was cleared for Vera Cruz, Mexico but refused her the right to land, she then sailed to Campeachy, Havana, and returned to New York in August with a load of log wood.

The sloop TRIO of 160 tons was built at Elizabethtown, New Jersey 1795 and registered 30 May 1795 New York, registered in Connecticut 4 July 1796, owner and master Ezra Hubbell. She cleared New York 19 July 1796 for St Bartholomew and was in port

---

[58] *Commercial Advertiser* 23 August 1798.

[59] *Commercial Advertiser* 20 December 1798.

[60] Bown, pp 170-181.

Guadalupe 23 August. She returned to New York via Boston 14 October 1796. She was in port Charleston December 1796 to January 1797.

The sloop CORNELIA was built in 1797 Huntington, Connecticut and registered 1797-1798 in Newfield. She was 50 tons, length 56 feet 1 inch, draft 6 feet 13 inches, beam 19 feet, with 1 mast and a square stern. Her master was Thaddeus Hubbell in 1797 and possibly later Wilson Hubbell. After visits to Norfolk, Charleston, and Jamaica in April 1798, she arrived in New York in May. Two hours after leaving Jamaica, she was boarded by an English schooner of 14 guns. The English schooner had recently been engaged with a French privateer but she escaped with the loss of 2 officers. The CORNELIA left New York in May for Philadelphia and was then cleared for Exuma. Exuma is an island in the Bahamas, settled by American loyalists in 1783.

The sloop EXPERIMENT of Stratford was built in 1799 at Huntington and registered at Stratford 1799-1800. She was 53 tons, length 55 feet, draft 6 feet 5 inches beam 17 feet 9 inches, 1 mast, and a square stern. Ezra Hubbell (365) was master in 1799. She sailed from Newfield for the West Indies and was wrecked at 5 March 1800. The captain and crew were picked up and carried into Norfolk. Ezra was lost at sea September 1804.

The brig GOOD HOPE was recorded in a single arrival at Philadelphia from Jamaica 10 October 1795 with a cargo of sugar in hogsheads, coffee in hogsheads, high proof spirits, logwood and hides.

The brig INDEPENDENCE was built at Stratford, registered at Bridgeport and Newfield from 1800 to 1805. She was 88 tons, length 64 feet 2 inches, draft 7 feet 8 inches, beam 21 feet 3 inches with 2 masts and a round tuck stern. Her 1802 registry at Bridgeport says she is owned by Thaddeus Hubbell, Davis Sterling, James E. Beach, Silas Sherman and Daniel Fayerweather, merchants. The master was

Chapter 8

Thaddeus Hubbell. She was first noted on 5 July 1797 when she arrived in Newfield from St. John capital of Antigua, an island in the West Indies, with rum, molasses, sugar and fruit for which she paid a duty of $1,856.[61] On 1 October she again arrived in Newfield with salt and fruit. On 2 July 1800 when she arrived in New York from Exuma. She arrived again on 1 October when she completed a 20 day voyage from Exuma. She made the trip regularly from Exuma or New Providence, Bahamas from 1801 to 1804. On October 12, 1801 she landed a cargo of salt. 19 March 1802 her cargo was mahogany, lignumvitae (a hard, heavy wood used for pulleys), and fustick, a tropical wood. June 1802 was another cargo of salt. In February 1803 she was unable to make port for 10 days due to adverse winds and thick weather. April 1804 she was boarded by the British sloop of war CONQUE and 10 French soldiers were put on board without any provisions. Previous to this the CONQUE and taken the ship MARY ANN of Boston from St. Domingo, Dominican Republic with 500 French soldiers onboard, the CONQUE distributed them on board every American vessel she came across. The INDEPENDENCE was last noted arriving in New York 27 November 1804.

The sloop DELANCY of Bridgeport was 55 tons, length 56 feet 7 inches, draft 6 feet 3 inches, beam 18 feet 7 inches with a square stern. She was registered 28 January 1802, owner and master Ezra Hubbell. She arrived in New York from Guadalupe (Guadeloupe) and St. Thomas in April 1802 with a cargo of sugar and coffee. Guadeloupe is in the Leeward Islands, Lesser Antilles and prominent in the sugar trade. St. Thomas is in the Virgin Islands. She sailed again for New Providence and returned to New York in June. DELANCY left Bridgeport for Charleston in October 1802, arriving on the 19th.

Little is known of the ANN except for a single trip from Philadelphia to St Domingo in March 1805.

---

[61] Knapp p. 120.

Chapter 8

The 100 ton brig WILLIAM (1) was registered on 7 October 1805 by owner Thaddeus Hubbell. She is registered with master Thaddeus Hubbell in 1807, 15 May 1809 and 14 May 1810. She engaged in the West Indies trade and averaged a round trip a month from 1805 to 1810. 14 December 1805 she arrived in New York from New Providence with a cargo of salt, sugar and molasses. April 10, 1806 she arrived at Bridgeport from Nassau with a cargo of sugar. She was captured by the British frigate ISTAR, Captain Cramer 30 November 1806 at Point Mount, Africa, and Captain Hubbell was picked up by the United States schooner CAROLINA. March 9th 1807 she arrived in New York with a cargo of Cayenne pepper, pimento and Race Ginger. In 1807, Captain Hubbell offered for sale a few tons of Nicaraguan wood, one large anchor and some old copper. She arrived at Bridgeport from New Providence with a cargo of molasses and sugar 26 October 1807. Cargoes carried on the WILLIAM also included Spanish segars, muscovado sugar, white sugar, Virginia Flour, caster (castor) oil, cotton, mahogany, log wood, Maderia wine, snuff, salt, cocoa, molasses and rose leaves. She continued the West Indies trade to October 1810. Elijah Kirtland husband of Sarah Hubbell Kirtland (1003) died at sea on the brig WILLIAM November 1810. WILLIAM was last registered in 1810. On 10 November WILLIAM cleared Bridgeport for New Providence under command of Captain Stephen Summers and was never seen again.

The schooner HANNAH ANN, Captain Gershom Hubbell arrived in New York 22 January 1806 after a 20 day voyage from Guadalupe. This is probably Gershom E. Hubbell (1018, 1788-1859) but he was just 18 years old.

The armed schooner COMMERCE (1) called of Kennebec sailed from Savannah for Jamaica May 1798 and was spoken to at latitude 30 longitude 74 6 days from Savanna.

The Schooner COMMERCE (2) was 130 tons and built at Saybrook, Connecticut, registered 28 November 1803. Probably under Captain Benjamin Hubbell, she sailed for Havana in the spring of 1806 returning to New York with a cargo of log wood, sugar & coffee. In May 1806 she prepared to get under way for Havana:

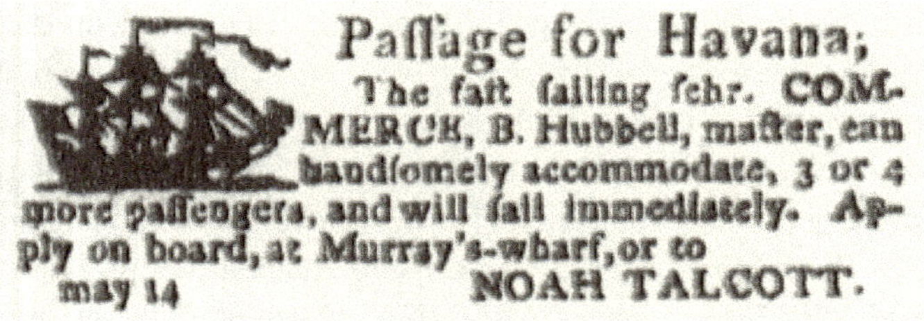
Paſſage for Havana;
The faſt ſailing ſchr. COMMERCE, B. Hubbell, maſter, can handſomely accommodate, 3 or 4 more paſſengers, and will ſail immediately. Apply on board, at Murray's-wharf, or to
may 14 NOAH TALCOTT.

Figure 23 *New York Gazette* 14 May 1806. Early American Newspapers. op. cit.

She was bound for St Johns in 1806 with a load of cedar when she was intercepted and captured by a Spanish privateer and condemned on account of short clearance (not all cargo listed on the manifest) for having 200 boxes of sugar not cleared and tobacco which was prohibited. She was bought by Mr. Sage of Savannah and when going out of the harbor was run ashore by the pilot where she lay for 17 hours in a dangerous situation. She was carried to St. Augustine by the Spanish privateer BON UNION, Captain Pealy.

The first HOPE (1) was a sloop of Newfield CT built in 1793. She was 86 tons, length 63 feet 3 inches, beam 20 feet 7 inches, draft 7 feet 10 inches, 1 deck, 1 mast and a square stern. Salmon Hubbell was master 6 September 1794.

The second HOPE (2) was a schooner first noted in November 1810 when she arrived in Charleston from Martinique. Four day later on 18 November, she cleared for Martinique, St Kitts and St Pierre arriving back in Charleston the end of December. St Kitts is an island in the Leeward Islands and St Pierre was an important city of Martinique until destroyed by a volcanic eruption in 1902. During this voyage she had to put into St Kitts for repairs when her main mast was carried away. She made 3 more trips to Martinique in the spring of 1811.

Chapter 8

Sloop FARMER was built in Stratford 1794 and registered in Newfield and Stratford 1794-1801. She was 67 tons, length 60 feet 10 inches, draft 6 feet 11 inches, beam 19 feet, with 1 mast and a square stern. The master was Thaddeus Hubbell. One voyage has been found when it was reported that she arrived in Newfield from Nassau, Bahamas on 24 December 1799.

The following is yet to be resolved:

"DANBURY, Nov. 18.
We learn from Newfield, that a sloop commanded by Capt. Hubble of that place, foundered on her passage from the West-Indies (by splitting open) a Mr. Wakely and a negro man were lost with the sloop and a very valuable cargo, consisting, in part of 2200 bushels of salt, and several hogheads of molasses. The Capt and rest of the crew saved themselves by means of the boat, and were taken up and carried into New-York, after having endured all the hardships of being at sea in an open boat for six days, without any necessary of life, save half a biscuit each, per day"[62]

The brig POLLY (2) of Charleston, master Sears Hubbell (491, 1777-1838) arrived in Charleston from Campeachy 27 Aug 1806. The town of Campeche, Mexico is in the Gulf of Campeche. In September the POLLY was blown off course when returning from Campeachy and put into Tybee, an island off Georgia, finally arriving in Charleston on 8 September with 15 survivors who were adrift for 11 days from the schooner LITTLE PATTY which was wrecked in the gale of 27 August.

". . . Charleston, Sept. 6. Last evening came up to town, in a pilot boat, capt G Geere, of the sch. Little Patty, which was wrecked in the gale on the 22d Aug. and Mr. John Curtis, a passenger; who, with 15 others, after drifting in an open boat, destitute of food, sails, oars, and every other necessary article for eleven days and nights, were fortunately picked up on the 2d of September by capt. Hubble, of the brig Polly, from Campeachy bound to this port"[63]

Captain Hubbell and the POLLY left Charleston for Laguna, departing that port on 19 December she was intercepted by the British frigate ORPHEUS and succeeded in retaking the brig. The

---

[62] Essex Journal 4 December 1793
[63] *Freemans's Friend* 27 September 1306

Chapter 8

last recorded voyage was when she arrived in Charleston from 1 January 1808.

"Two days after leaving Laguna, captain Hubbell was boarded by the British frigate Orpheus, captain Brigs, who detained his papers six hours, and then sent an officer and six men on board the brig, took out all his crew, and without assigning any cause ordered her for Jamaica. Off cape Florida captain Hubbell, with the assistance of his mate, succeeded in retaking the brig"[64]

The brig ARGONAUT was built in 1800 at Huntington, Connecticut and registered from 1801 to 1804 at Bridgeport. She was 80 tons, length 61 feet, draft 7 feet 6 inches beam 20 feet 6 inches. She had two masts and a square stern. Ezra Hubbell was master in 1800. She sailed from New Orleans to Havana and then to Philadelphia in the fall of 1811 under the command of Benjamin Hubbell with a cargo of cotton and lead.

The VENUS was reported as both a sloop and as a schooner owned and sailed by Ezra Hubbell. She arrived in New York 16 June 1804 from New Providence and travelled to West Indies again in August.

NOTE: There are 3 possibly 4 different vessels under Captain Hubbell with the name EAGLE. Two others are discussed in Chapters 5 and 9.

The first EAGLE is a sloop built in 1794 at Fairfield and registered at Newfield. She was 74 tons, length 59 feet 6 inches, draft 7 feet 3 inches, beam 20 feet 7 inches with one mast and a quarter stern with badges. From 1795 to 1796 the owner was Thaddeus Hubbell and she was registered 3 February 1795 with master Thaddeus Hubbell and again on 15 June 1795. She sailed from Oporto 13 February 1794 with a cargo of salt for Philadelphia arriving on 9 April 1794 (she was called a ship). She arrived in New York from St. Croix, Virgin Islands 11 May 1795 and proceeded to Bridgeport. During this voyage, a passenger died in the West Indies. In September 1795 she left Bridgeport for St Thomas and arrived in Norfolk in February

---

[64] *National Intelligencer* 14 January 1807.

Chapter 8

1796. Another voyage recorded in May 1795 departed Newfield to New York, St. Croix and back to New York. *Greenleaf's New York Journal* of 13 May 1795 lists schooner EAGLE, Hubble from St. Croix and sloop EAGLE, Hubbell, from St. Croix. Thaddeus Hubbell and the EAGLE made at least 2 more trips finally arriving in Norfolk 24 February 1796.

The ship POLLY & BETSEY of New York Captain Bird sailed from Martinique about November 12th but was chased by a French privateer and made for Dominico.

"Baltimore, Dec 13 . . . . While examining captain Bird, the ship Polly and Betsey, of New-York, Capt E Hubbell who had sailed in company with him from Martinique, hove in sight, and seeing the privateer board the Charlotte, bore up for Dominique the privateer immediately gave chase, and when Capt Bird last saw them they were close under Dominique and the privateer nearly up with them". [65]

This period of growth and high commercial activity was about to be abruptly effected by war.

---

[65] *Polar-Star* 26 Dec 1796.

Chapter 8

A fully rigged ship
Figure 24. publicdomainvectors.org

UNNAMED VESSELS (5)

This report was a mystery for some time. A small shallop with a cargo
of pottery on board drifted into Oysterbay with no one on board.
Papers on board indicated that the master was Zachariah Hubbel and
the owner was James Ingram. The date was 30 September 1751 and
the newspaper account was 7 October 1751. According to the 1995
Additions and Corrections to the History and Genealogy of the
Hubbell Family, there are only 2 know Hubbell's named Zachariah
and one was born after 1751. See page 5

Chapter 9

War of 1812

In 1807, Great Britain was at war with Napoleon. In order to pay for the war, all merchant vessels trading with France were stopped at sea and required to pay a tax on all goods bound for France. Additionally, the British had difficulty providing crew for their warships. When a vessel under neutral colors such as the United States was stopped by the British, crew members were lined up and any with a British accent were impressed into Royal Navy service as suspected deserters. About six thousand were removed from American commercial vessels. After a narrow vote in Congress, war was declared. The war was not popular in New England since a great deal of trade was conducted with the British. By 1814 wharfs were abandoned and commerce was dead. Peace was signed in 1815.[66]

Most merchants were very conservative, slow to adapt new technologies, and very protective. They were very reluctant to risk lives, profits or savings on new inventions at all times but particularly during the War of 1812. Nevertheless the demands for goods continued and risks were taken. Hubbell trading firms thrived.

The firm Smith & Hubbell operated from 1810 to1819. The partners Joseph Smith and Anson Hubbell (376, 1787-1819) were based in New York on South Street. Anson was the son of Captain Amos Hubbell (117) and his second wife Eleanor Hubbell (493) daughter of Nathan Hubbell (159) and Anna Wakeman, "his second cousin, once removed".[67]

"25 May 1810. The subscribers being entered into co-partnership, their business will be conducted with the firm SMITH & HUBBELL at 45 South St. Joseph R. Smith & Anson Hubbell."

The firm handled cargoes from all over the world i.e. Havana, Cuba; Bordeaux, France; Port au Prince and Aux Cays, Haiti; Algeciras and

---

[66] PBS, 10 October 2011, "The War of 1812",
[67] HBC p174.

Chapter 9

Cadiz, Spain; Liverpool, England; Lisbon, Portugal; Fayal, Azores; Calcutta and Madras, India; et al. The cargoes were as varied as the ports, some samples; quick silver, Hyson tea, Bohea tea, goat skins, livestock (Merino sheep), Bourbon coffee, indigo, sugar, gin, cedar, Naples brandy, flats for hats, fruit, Malaga wine, Madeira wine, specie, pig iron, rum, silk, turtle shells, claret, oranges, limes, salt, ginger and a 300 ton anchor. They also charted and sold vessels. George William Hubbell (1341, 1796-1831), the eldest son of Captain Ezekiel Hubbell and Catharine joined the firm at the age of sixteen. When he was nineteen he was employed by the firm as supercargo (see terms) on the brig CANNON on a voyage to Portugal and Gibraltar. In 1816 he was supercargo for a load of munitions to Buenos Aires, then fighting for independence from Spain. There was an oversupply and after some time George W. Hubbell sold the ship and cargo at a loss. The partnership ended with the death of Anson Hubbell 7 September 1819. George William Hubbell went on to be the Consul General in the Philippines where he died of cholera in 1831.

Hubbell & Waters traded between Philadelphia and Baltimore about 1812 to 1817. The company traded flax, buttons, rum, sugar, fruit, coffee, earthenware, and snuff. The 1812 directory for Baltimore lists Hubbell & Waters, merchants, County wharf, Captain Josiah Hubbell (688, 1788-?) merchant 54 Hanover St. They also dealt with slaves, in June 1812 they offered for sale a negro girl about 17 years of age, a good cook and washer. In December they offered three young Negro boys and one Negro girl.

The sloop ANTOINETTE of Bridgeport, owned Gershom E. Hubbell, (1018) was a 69 ton sloop built in Connecticut and enrolled 17 Nov 1813. She sailed from Bridgeport to Boston 18 November 1811 and New Haven to New York September 1813 with a load of salt.

The schooner AMANDA made at least 7 successful round trips from New York to Washington, North Carolina and return. On the last trip,

Chapter 9

7 days out of New York and bound for Wilmington, North Carolina she was wrecked on 27 February 1812 at latitude 38 longitude 69. Captain Abraham Hubbe_ (508, 1786-1819), his wife and crew were rescued by the brig R-STATES, Captain Blanchard, and arrived in Portsmouth, New Hampshire 12 March 1812.

The third EAGLE is the schooner which made the New York to Washington, North Carolina voyage and return with Naval stores at least 16 times from July 1814 to August 1817.

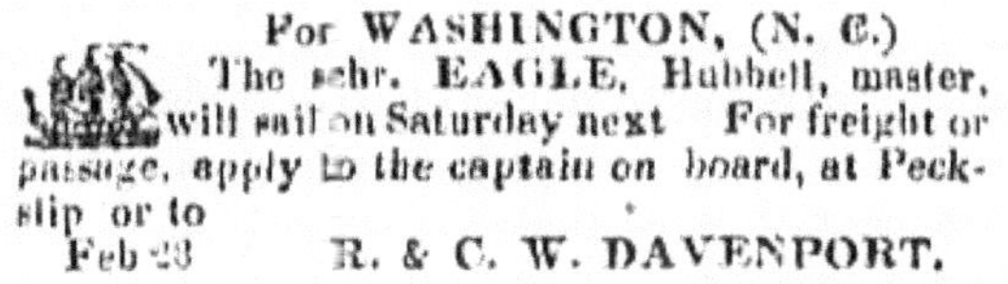

For WASHINGTON, (N. C.)
The schr. EAGLE, Hubbell, master, will sail on Saturday next   For freight or passage, apply to the captain on board, at Peck-slip or to
Feb 28   R. & C. W. DAVENPORT.

Figure 25. *The Evening Post* 2 March 1816. Early American Newspapers. op. cit.

The schooner ELIZA (2) arrived in New York from Wilmington, North Carolina 18 July 1814 with a cargo of tar and spirits of turpentine. On 25 June off Cape Hatteras she was boarded by a pilot boat and informed that the light in the light house at Cape Hatteras was out because there was no oil for the lamp.

The brig GEORGE WASHINGTON of 76 tons was built at Washington, North Carolina in 1811 and enrolled 18 September 1811. She made at least one trip from Washington to New York arriving 10 June 1812.

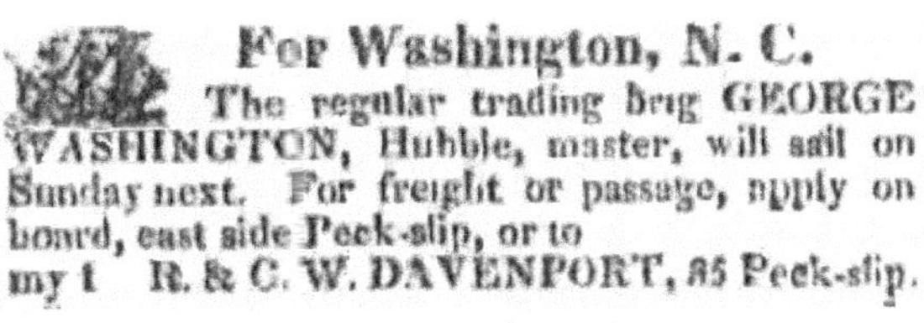

For Washington, N. C.
The regular trading brig GEORGE WASHINGTON, Hubble, master, will sail on Sunday next. For freight or passage, apply on board, east side Peck-slip, or to
my 1   R. & C. W. DAVENPORT, 85 Peck-slip.

Figure 26. *New York Gazette* 2 May 1812. Early American Newspapers. op. cit.

The brig LEOPARD was built in 1812 at Bridgeport and registered from 1815 to 1826 at Bridgeport. She was 168 tons, length 80 feet 10

Chapter 9

inches, draft 10 feet 6 ½ inches, beam 24 feet 3 inches with 2 masts, a square stern, with a leopard figurehead. Part owner and master was Thaddeus Hubbell. The LEOPARD was noted in West Indies trade from 1815 to 1820. Ports of call included Antigua, St Pierre's, Martinique, Lisbon, St Ubes, Leeward Islands, St Croix, St Eustatica and St Barthomew. In July 1815 she arrived in New York with a cargo of rum, sugar and molasses. In May 1816 she left Bridgeport for Lisbon and spent June and July trying to sell her cargo. She returned to Bridgeport in August and resumed her more lucrative West Indies trade, completing more than a dozen trips until 1820.

The brig LYON arrived in New London from Bridgeport 6 December 1815.

The schooner ELIZA (2) arrived in New York from Wilmington, North Carolina 18 July 1814 with a cargo of tar and spirits of turpentine.

The schooner MARY (3) sailed between New York, Bridgeport, Boston and Philadelphia from 1813 to 1815. Her master was Gershom E. Hubbell in 1813. Her cargoes consisted of corn, tea, rum and sugar.

The MARY GORHAM cleared Boston for Bridgeport 26 December 1815. This ship could possibly be confused with schooner MARY (3).

Sears Hubbell was the master of the ship ROBERT in port Portsmouth 15 March 1812. She was next observed in New York in July 1812 preparing to sail to London and completed the trip at Charleston on 21 October 1812. During that trip on 18 September she was boarded by the British frigate SYBELLE at latitude 44 longitude 30 and treated politely. On 16 October she encountered a severe gale and the fore and main mast and jib boom were carried away. A libel suit was filed against the cargo and the ship.

"Marine Register

Chapter 9

PORT OF CHARLESTON
ARRIVED

Ship Robert, Hubbell, London, 50 days. Goods (full) to Kohne & Maxwell, and others. September 18, lat. 44, long. 30, was boarded by the British frigate Sybelle, the Fortune in company and treated politely – they informed that they had captured on the 13th, the brig Warren, Cook, from Providence, (a.i.) bound to Lisbon and ordered her for Cork, where the frigates were bound – Oct. 16, lat.33, 15, long. 59, experienced a very severe gale from S.E. during which the Robert had her fore and main top masts and jib boom carried away; it blew a complete hurricane for about three hours; the ship lost a great part of her sails, rigging and spars, and was much injured in her Hull, &c. On Monday evening, off Cape Romain, was boarded by the British brig Rhodian, after making us haul down our colours, she fired a shot which came over the quarter deck, Just above the passengers heads – the capt was ordered on board with his papers, which were examined very closely . . .[68]

"IN THE ADMIRALTY
UNITED STATES OF AMERICA
South Carolina District.
By virtue of a precept to me directed, issued out of the Court aforesaid, I do hereby cite and admonish all person having any right or title in or to certain GOODS, WARES and MERCHANDIZE, imported in the ship Robert, Sears Hubbell master, against which a libel has been exhibited and filed in this honorable Court, to be an appear at the Court House in Charleston, on FRIDAY, the 13th November, at eleven o'clock in the forenoon, to shew cause if any they can, why the prayer of the said libel should not be granted.
Robert E. Cochran, Marshal October 22"[69]

"IN THE ADMIRALTY
UNITED STATES OF AMERICA
South Carolina District.
By virtue of a precept to me directed, issued out of the Court aforesaid, I do hereby cite and admonish all person having any right or title in or to certain in or to the ship Robert, her Tackle, Apparel and Furniture, Sears Hubbell, master . . .[70]

The 107 ton schooner SALLY/SALLY ANN was built in Derby 1811 and owned by Charles B. Hubbell (377) et al, Thaddeus Hubbell was master. On 31 May 1812 she was observed at latitude 41.30 longitude 49.13 and arrived 15 June 1812 at Bridgeport after a 38 day voyage from Figueira with salt and fruit. She was one of very

---

[68] *The Investigator* 21 October 1912.

[69] *City Gazette* 22 October 1812.

[70] *City Gazette* 23 October 1812 .

Chapter 9

few vessels to arrive during the War of 1812. Her list of six owners probably reflects a means of spreading wartime risks.[71]

SOLYMA/SALOMA, a schooner was taken in possession by a large ship of war off Currituck and sent to Bermuda 19 Jan 1813.

For Washington, N. C.
The sch'r SALOMA, Hubbell, master will sail on Wednesday next. For freight of passage apply on board, east side Peck-slip, or to
R. & C. W. DAVENPORT,
N30   35 Peck-slip.

Figure 27. *New York Gazette* 30 November 1812. Early American Newspapers. op. cit.

The schooner WILLIAM HULL (sometimes reported as WILLIAM) of Charleston first appears in November 1813 arriving in Charleston from Havana. Captain Hubbell was cosignee for a cargo of sugar and coffee December 1813. She was called a pilot boat schooner. She made the trip at least 4 more times until May 1814 when she was captured.

"Charleston, May 23. BRITISH FLEET IN THE OFFING.
A British frigate appeared in this offing yesterday, with a white flag flying at her fore-topmast, and last evening she sent a boat into Rebellion Roads, and put on board the U.S. schooner Carolina, lying at anchor there, Capt. Hubbell, late master of the pilot boat schooner William, of this port, which vessel was captured on Thursday last, in 18 fathoms water, on her passage from Havana, with a cargo of sugar, coffee, &c. and order for the West Indies. Captain H. was treated with much politeness while onboard the frigate, the commander of which put himself to some inconvenience in order to land Captain H. and two gentlemen who were passengers on board his schooner. . . Charleston, May 24. Since our last, we have conversed with Captain Hubbell, of the schooner William, mentioned in yesterday's Courier, as having been captured on Thursday last, off this port by a British frigate. Captain H. informs us that the frigate is the Ister, Capt Cramer . . . Captain Hubbell was informed by the Captain of the Ister, that before he left the West Indies news had been received of the capture of Bordeaux by the army of Lord Wellington. . ."[72]

---

[71] Knapp p. 121.
[72] *Daily National Intelligencer* 31 May 1814.

61

Chapter 9

February 9, 1815 she arrived in Charleston from New Orleans via Havana and reported on the Battle of New Orleans.

"FROM HAVANNA.
Charleston, Feb 8.
By the arrival of the schr. William Hull, capt Hubbell, we learn, that accounts had been received there from the British army, near New Orleans, to the 17th of January. They confirm the news which had already reached us form other quarters, of the complete defeat of the British on the 8th ult. There were at Havanna, when capt H arrived there, a 64 gun ship, 2 frigates and 2 brigs, the first mentioned had come with orders to purchase 3000 bbls of flour and had bought and taken on board 2000 barrels, when another brig arrived, and immediately after communicating with the 64, they all got underway, excepting one frigate and proceeded for New Orleans. From their going off in so great a hurry, it was presumed that the British were fearful of being cut off by the Americans, and were about to withdraw their army.
It was difficult to obtain information from the British officers at Havanna, relative to their operations, but from what leaked out, it was evident they had suffered dreadfully, not only by the sword, but by the inclemency of the season. A great number of British troops are said to have perished with the cold, and many of the officers on board the ships at Havanna were frostbitten. From the best information that could be obtained it was believed, that the British had not lost from the time of their landing up to the 17th ult. from all causes, less than 5000 men. A British officer admitted to Capt H that they lost 30 barges in the attack upon our gun boats – our men, to use his own expression, fought like 'bulldogs,' and, of 140 men belonging to his vessel which went into the action, 30 only came out uninjured. . ."[73]

The sloop LIBERTY arrived in New York 3 days from Richmond 21 August 1815.

The 66 ton sloop VICTRESS, Charles B. Hubbell (377, 1789-1873) was part owner and master in 1814. Later, he had interests in the 67 ton sloop BRIDGEPORT, 21 ton sloop INTREPID and the 93 ton schooner ANN MARIA.[74] He was master of the LAPWING covered in Chapter 10.

---

[73] *Daily National Intelligencer* 21 February 1815.
[74] Knapp p. 122.

Chapter 9

The great September gale of 1815, first hurricane to hit New England in 180 years came ashore at Long Island on 23 September 1815 and then hit Saybrook, Connecticut.

Ships at sea
Figure 28 publicdomainvectors.org

Chapter 10

Age of Optimism

The Navigation Act of 1817 prohibited foreign trade between one American port and another caused the coastal trade to flourish. Overseas trade was energetic with American merchants active around the world. January 11th, 1826 George Hubbell arrived in New York from Cadiz, Spain, That same year on February 14th, A. Hubbell, merchant. arrived in New York from Bremen, Germany.

The newly rebuilt CITIZEN is mentioned again in January 1818 when she cleared New York for the East Indies, again under the command of Ezekiel Hubbell who came out of retirement after nine years. She was sighted in the Straights of Sunda in May and arrived in Manila in June 141 days out of New York. She sailed for Canton, returning via Manila and arriving in New York April 1819.

UGARS, INDIGO, &c.—Now landing at pier No 13, East River, from the ship Citizen, E. Hubbell, master, from Manilla
7000 small bags Manilla Sugars, being all of the first quality and well selected
25 cases Indigo, 166 tanned Hides
150 piculs of Sabeco Dye Wood
1 case Rattan Hats
9 bales Grass Matts, for sale by
a 15 3t   HOYT & TOM, 45 South-st.

Figure 29. *Mercantile Advertiser* 17 April 1819. Early American Newspapers. op. cit.

The CITIZEN was again dispatched to Manila in 1819 under the command of Captain James Loring with Ezekiel's son George William Hubbell as supercargo. At Manila he purchased a cargo for Europe and arrived in Hamburg in May 1820 where he left the ship and returned to New York. The CITIZEN was wrecked on the New Jersey coast in 1822.

"SHIPWRECK. – The ship Citizen, Loring, 256 days from Manilla, with a cargo of 9570 bags sugar, to Hoyt Tom, owner, was cast away about 8 o'clock last Tuesday morning on Brigantine Shoal, opposite Absecom Inlet, in a gale from E.N.E. When she struck endeavored to wear around, but she still hung on; then hove all aback, but to no purpose, and she beat over the shoal early in the

Chapter 10

morning and sunk in about 5 fathoms of water. Captain Loring and crew were taken off by the schr Union, Mersereau, of Staten Island and landed at Absecom."[75]

The ship AJAX was newly constructed and registered in New York 14 April 1821. Ezekiel Hubbell supervised her construction, and sailed in her as master, from New York to Manila in 1821. During the first voyage to Manila, the rudder was knocked off in a severe storm 17 October 1821. The AJAX returned from Manila 15 May 1822 with a cargo of sugar and coffee. After one month, Ezekiel again left New York for Manila 17 June 1822 and arrived in Manila 20 December 1822. He left his two sons George William and Henry Wilson in Manila with a view to establishing a mercantile house. The business was organized on the First of January 1822 under the name George W. Hubbell. The firm continued under the name Peele, Hubbell & Co. for many years. George later became the United States Consul in the Philippines. See Annex B & C. The AJAX returned to New York 29 April 1823. Typically, each leg of the voyage lasted about 128 days. The third voyage commenced 2 June 1823 when Ezekiel sailed from New York, arriving in Manila 20 December 1823 and returning to New York 25 April 1824. The fourth and last voyage departed New York 26 May 1824 and arrived in Manila 10 December 1824. He arrived in New York 22 May 1825 with a cargo of coffee, sugar, tortoise, pearl shells, wax plaintain (sic) bark, 8000 bags of sugar and 164 cases of indigo. Ezekiel then sold the AJAX and she floundered in August 1825 during a voyage to England. Ezekiel had two more voyages before retirement. The brig ALONZO sailed from New Orleans 1 August 1817 with a cargo of cotton and hides. After 30 days from New Orleans and 28 days from Belize she arrived at New York 31 August 1817.

The sloop BELL/BELLE (2) was owned by Josiah Hubbell and Gershom E. Hubbell was master. April 1820 she made the voyage from Bridgeport to Boston with 1600 bushels corn, 300 bushels rye, 2 sacks of feathers, 500 lbs of flax and 50 corn bags. She made another round trip in May and in June from Boston to New York with 1600

---

[75] *Baltimore Patriot* 15 April 1822.

Chapter 10

bushels corn, 400 bushels rye and 100 bushels of oats. In August she
sailed from Salem to New York with pepper and rum. In September
she again made the trip to Boston with 2000 bushels of corn, 100
bushels rye and 100 bushels oats. In February 1821 she arrived in
Boston with gin, raisins, dye woods and shoes. He made three more
trips that year and in October 1823 the BELLE had sprung a leak and
was expected to be condemned as unseaworthy.

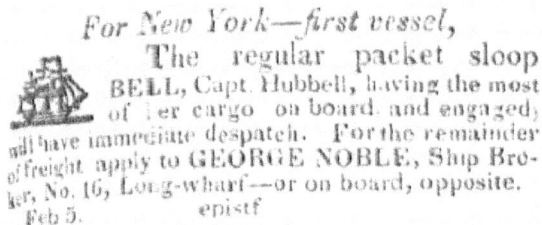

For New York—first vessel,

The regular packet sloop
BELL, Capt. Hubbell, having the most
of her cargo on board, and engaged,
will have immediate despatch. For the remainder
of freight apply to GEORGE NOBLE, Ship Bro-
ker, No. 16, Long-wharf—or on board, opposite.
Feb 5.   epistf

Figure 30. *Boston Daily Advertiser* 5 February 1821. Early American Newspapers op. cit.

With over 125 references in newspapers, schooner CARPENTER'S
SON and Captain Hubbell, probably Abraham Hubbell (509. 1786-
1819) are mentioned more often than any other ship/captain
combination encountered during this research. She was probably built
in Swansboro, North Carolina in 1810 and enrolled 25 January 1817
in New York. During Captain Hubbell's tenure, she made over 70
round trips between New York and the southern port of Washington,
North Carolina with rare trips to Boston and Wilmington. The house
of R. & C. Davenport & Co. handled the disposition of the cargo in
New York. Each leg of the trip averaged 7 days, from December
1816 to October 1819. Usually she carried naval stores consisting of
tar, resin and turpentine with occasional cargoes of furs, flex seed and
tobacco. October 7th 1819 she arrived at the Port of New York,
Captain Hubbell died the next day at the Marine Hospital, Staten
Island. After the death of Captain Hubbell, The CARPENTER'S
SON continued the route under Captains Prescott and Etheridge
sponsored by Cambrelong & Pearson. See Annex A.

Chapter 10

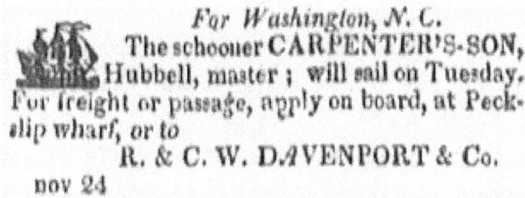

For Washington, N. C.
The schooner CARPENTER'S-SON,
Hubbell, master ; will sail on Tuesday.
For freight or passage, apply on board, at Peck-
slip wharf, or to
R. & C. W. DAVENPORT & Co.
nov 24

Figure 31. *Evening Post* 24 November 1817. Early American Newspapers. op. cit.

Schooner CATCH ME IF YOU CAN made one trip from Boston to New York in April 1818 with a cargo of rum and fish.

The GENERAL WALE was cleared at New Orleans July 1816 for a voyage to Porto Rico.

A brief mention of the DOVE occurred in January 1817 when she was cleared for a trip to Washington (NC?).

The sloop COMMODORE PATTERSON (1) of New Orleans was built in Baltimore in 1816. She was 83 tons, length 64 feet 6 inches, beam 19 feet 7 inches, draft 7 feet 10 inches, one deck, one mast, square stern and round tuck. Her master was Julius Hubbell (1115, 1787-1837). She was reported as a brig in New Orleans 12 December 1819 when she sailed for Havana, returning to New Orleans in January 1820 after a 3 day sail from Nuevitas. She arrived in New Orleans 11 April 1820 and was scheduled to sail for Havana on 26 of April. She cleared on 3 May, arriving on 11 May.

The schooner DECATUR was probably built in 1816 at Orrington, Maine. She was 65 tons, 63 feet length, 18 feet beam and with a draft of 7 feet. Her owner was Charles B. Hubbell and her master Gersham E. Hubbell. From March 1816 to July 1818 she made numerous trips between Boston, New York and Bridgeport carrying a cargo of rye, corn, oats, molasses, beef, cider, flax, fish, leather, flour, rum and dry goods.

Chapter 10

N. E. RUM.

LANDING this day at Burling-slip, from on board the schr. Decatur, Hubbell, master, from Boston, 18 hhds. N. E. RUM

For sale by D'WOLF, PACKARD & D'WOLF,

apl 4 41 South-treet.

Figure 32. *Commercial Advertiser* 8 April 1816, Early American Newspapers. op. cit.

The sloop FLORET made round trips from Bridgeport to Boston from December 1818 to July 1821 under owner and master Gershom E. Hubbell. The trip usually took 2 days and the cargo was grain, corn, rye, and oats. She could carry from 1200 to 1600 bushels of corn, 100 to 500 of bushels of rye, and between 100 to 300 bushels of oats. She usually tied up at Long wharf in Boston.

The HECTOR, a sloop of Bridgeport was owned by the merchant Richard Hubbell Jr. She cleared New Orleans in April 1818, sailed to Havana and then to Bridgeport. She arrived in Charleston with a load of 7 mules and northern produce in October 1821 and departed for Havana. She returned to Bridgeport 26 November 1821.

The schooner HENRIETTA cleared Washington, North Carolina for Guadalupe 12 May 1821 and returned 17 August. In October she arrived in Boston with a load of turpentine. In March 1822 she departed Washington, arriving in Baltimore on 5 April and Portsmouth, New Hampshire on 12 April.

The ISLINGTON a ship of New Orleans was built in Durham, New Hampshire 1812. She was 330 tons, length 102 feet 3 inches beam 27 feet, draft 12 feet with 2 decks, 3 masts and a square stern, her master was Julius Hubbell. She sailed from New Orleans to New York, arriving 23 June 1818 with a load of cotton and tobacco. The ISLINGTON cleared New York on 14 July and arrived in New Orleans 16 August. March 1819 she cleared New Orleans for Liverpool arriving 29 April and retuning to Philadelphia 23 July.

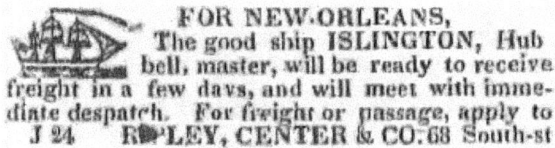

FOR NEW-ORLEANS,
The good ship ISLINGTON, Hubbell, master, will be ready to receive freight in a few days, and will meet with immediate despatch. For freight or passage, apply to
J 24   RIPLEY, CENTER & CO. 68 South-st

Figure 33. *Mercantile Advertiser* 29 June 1818. Early American Newspapers. op. cit.

The 19 ton sloop LAURA was registered in Derby from 1820 to 1822. Her master was Ezra Hubbell (645, 1776-) from 1820 to 1822. Also Norman Hubbell (1569, 1800-1875/9) but no date.

The brig LAURA ANN of 236 tons was built at Chatham, Connecticut in 1816 and enrolled at New York 29 October 1816. She is first noted in Havana July 1819 when loading. She arrived in Havana again 28 November 1819. She had sailed under Captain Norton but he was lost overboard in a September gale. She arrived in New York, Robert A. Hubbell (1696, 1799-1832) master 31 January 1820 with a cargo of fustic, coffee and honey. He also carried passengers of which 4 died on the voyage.[76]

The brig LEOPARD was built in 1812 at Bridgeport and registered from 1815 to 1826 at Bridgeport. She was 168 tons, length 80 feet 10 inches, draft 10 feet 6 ½ inches, beam 24 feet 3 inches. She had 2 masts a square stern, with a leopard figurehead. Thaddeus Hubbell was master and part owner along with Stephen Burroughs Jr. The LEOPARD was noted in West Indies trade from 1815 to 1820. Ports of call included Antigua, St Pierre's, Martinique, Lisbon, St Ubes, Leeward Islands, St Croix, St Eustatica and St Barthomew. In July 1815 she arrived in New York with a cargo of rum, sugar and molasses. 13 May 1815 Thaddeus left for Lisbon with a cargo of corn, staves, beef, mess pork, beans and white pine boards.[77] In May 1816 she left Bridgeport for Lisbon and spent June and July trying to sell her cargo. She returned to Bridgeport in August and resumed her more lucrative West Indies trade, completing more than a dozen trips until 1820. Ira Hubbell (1427, 1802-1865) almost died using charcoal

[76] NARA Film M237, Reel 1, List 22, Immigrant Ships Transcribers Guild.
[77] Knapp p. 122.

Chapter 10

in the hold of brig LEOPARD to kill rats 1 March 1821. Fortunately he was found unconscious and brought to fresh air. He was a seaman on the bark ALMERIA and died in Shanghai.[78]

The schooner MARTHA cleared New York for Havana 18 May 1816 and returned to Charleston 3 July. She made at least a dozen additional trips to Havana from 1816 to 1817. She delivered coffee and fruit to Charleston 20 August 1816, muscovado sugar, molasses and fruit 5 November 1816, and coffee 13 February 1817. She was last reported at Port au Prince 18 October 1817 when she put in to ask about markets. The MARTHA continued the Havana trade under other captains but was owned by Sears Hubbell (492, 1777-1838).

Prime Muscovado Sugar and retailing Molasses.
BY BOURS & BASCOME.
This Day, the 19th inst. will be sold on Lothrop's wharf, precisely at 12 o'clock,
The CARGO of the schooner MARTHA, Captain
Hubbell. from Havana, consisting of
61 hog-heads prime Retailing MOLASSES
3 tierces   ditto   ditto   ditto
13 tierces } Ditto Muscovado SUGAR.
60 barrels }
Conditions, cash.   November 19

Figure 34. *City Gazette* 19 November 1816. Early American Newspapers. op. cit.

SALES AT AUCTION.

PRIME GREEN COFFEE.
By Bours & Bascome.
This Day, 20th inst. will be sold on Lothrop's wharf, precisely at twelve o'clock, landing from the schooner Martha, Capt. Hubbell, from the Havana,
200 *bags prime Green Coffee.*
Conditions—cash for all sums of 500 dollars and under; above that amount, endorsed notes at sixty days.   February 20

Figure 35. *City Gazette* 20 February 1817. Early American Newspapers op. cit.

---

[78] E&R p 70.

Chapter 10

RAMBLER a brig out of New York cleared for Havana 15 January 1816.

The brig SEA GULL cleared Charleston for Madeira and Cadiz 11 March 1819 and arrived in Boston 5 June 1819 and then to Charleston. January 1820 she was in port at Cayenne to sail for Bueno Ayres. She arrived in distress on 22 December bound for Charleston being short of water and having lost more than half her cargo and most of her hay in 2 severe gales. April 5, 1820 she was at St Pierres arriving from Angostura with cattle to be delivered at St Lucia, and then to Charleston where she arrived 22 May 1820 with a cargo of sugar, cocoa, cloves and rum. On the Fourth of June 1820 the SEA GULL, Captain Hubbell, sailed from St Thomas.[79]

The brig WASHINGTON arrived in St Croix from Middletown 10 February 1817.

The second EAGLE is a schooner which made the New York to Washington, North Carolina voyage and return with Naval stores at least 16 times from July 1814 to August 1817. See Annex A for an analysis of these trips.

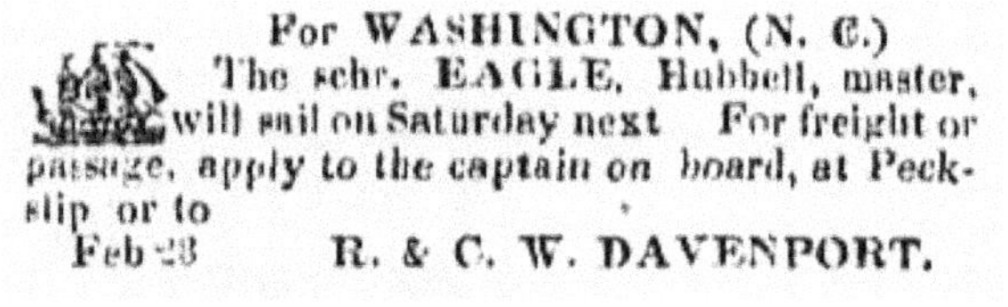

For WASHINGTON, (N. C.)
The schr. EAGLE, Hubbell, master, will sail on Saturday next For freight or passage, apply to the captain on board, at Peck-slip or to
Feb 28   R. & C. W. DAVENPORT.

Figure 36. *The Evening Post* 2 March 1816. Early American Newspapers. op. cit.

The sloop SPARTAN of 85 tons was built Killingsworth, Connecticut 1815 and enrolled in New York January. Charles B. Hubbell was the owner in 1818. She sailed from between Bridgeport, New York and Boston from October to November 1821, her cargo was molasses.

---

[79] *The New Times*, London 24 June 1820.

Chapter 10

The schooner UNION cleared New York for Savanna 23 August 1817 and arriving 2 September. She cleared Savanna on 4 September arriving at New York 22 September in ballast. She arrived in New York from Havana 2 May 1818 with a cargo of molasses, rum, sugar and tobacco. September 1818 she was up for sale.

FOR SAVANNAH,

The schr. Union, capt. Hubbel, loading east side Burling-slip; having her cargo mostly engaged, is intended to sail on Sunday next. For freight of the remainder, or passage, apply to capt. H. on board, or to
GRISWOLDS & COATES,
au 19   63 South-street·

Figure 37. *Evening Post* 19 Aug 1817. Early American Newspapers. op. cit.

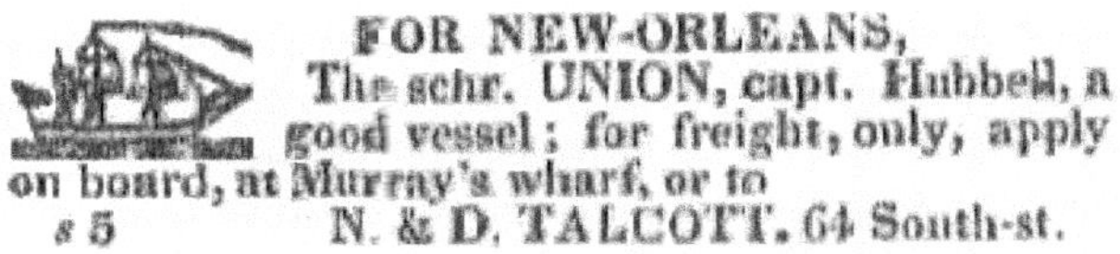

FOR NEW-ORLEANS,

The schr. UNION, capt. Hubbell, a good vessel; for freight, only, apply on board, at Murray's wharf, or to
s 5   N. & D. TALCOTT. 64 South-st.

Figure 38. *Mercantile Advertiser* 8 Sept 1818. Early American Newspapers. op. cit.

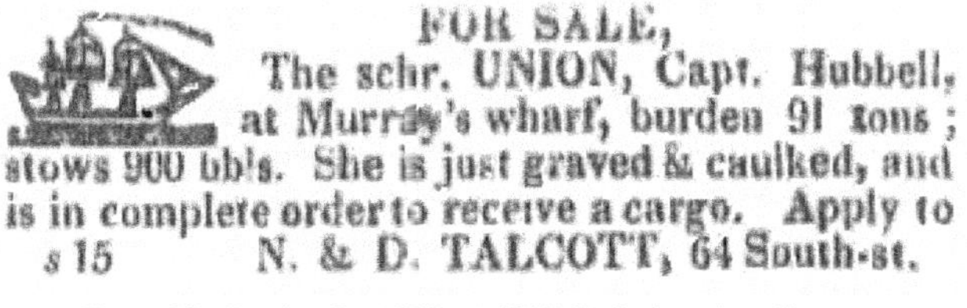

FOR SALE,

The schr. UNION, Capt. Hubbell, at Murray's wharf, burden 91 tons ; stows 900 bbls. She is just graved & caulked, and is in complete order to receive a cargo. Apply to
s 15   N. & D. TALCOTT, 64 South-st.

Figure 39. *Evening Post* 15 Sept 1818. **Early American Newspapers. op. cit.**

The sloop COMET was built during 1813 in Norwalk and registered in Norwalk and Bridgeport from 1813 to 1826. She was described as 49 tons, length 59 feet, draft 5 feet 1 inch, beam 19 feet 4 inches with one mast, a round tuck and a square stern. Joseph W. Hubbell was the master. She advertised packet service from Bridgeport to New York from April 1823 to June 1824.

Chapter 10

The 46 ton sloop LAPWING, Charles B. Hubbell (377) master and part owner arrived in Bridgeport 30 May 1821 and sailed the same day for New York. She left Bridgeport for Boston 25 July 1821. She arrived and sailed the same day from Bridgeport 5 September 1821 and arrived in Boston 15 September 1821. She sailed for Bridgeport 4 days later.

The ORION was a sloop built in 1818 at Norwalk and registered at Norwalk and Bridgeport from 1818 to 1841. She was 58 tons, length 51 feet 8 inches, draft 5 feet 5 inches, beam 19 feet 10 inches with a single mast, a round tuck, and a square stern. Masters were Joseph W. Hubbell (1009, 1800-1884), Mathias Hubbell and William L. Hubbell (1014, 1809-1843) The ORION made weekly runs from Bridgeport to New York and return, leaving Bridgeport on Tuesdays. A notice in June 1829 says the ORION will leave on Thursday, June 11, weather permitting.

A major change was on the horizon. It would take a long time to replace the sail but propulsion by steam was the future.

UNNAMED VESSELS (6)

A series of regular trips between Boston and New Haven took place between September 1770 and May 1773. No ship type, name or cargo is mentioned. The vessel was usually in and out of Boston on the same day. There is no reporting on the New Haven port. Master's name is Hubbell. Analysis suggests that this may be the SEA FLOWER or the SWALLOW.

Chapter 11

The End in Sight for Sail:
Wrecks, Wreckage and Romance. 1823-1840

The following was supplied by Margaret Brainard regarding John Hubbell (1597, 1803-1835) who married Mary Ann Hallock in 1825, she died in 1896. The obit of Mary Ann says,

" It was at the launching of a ship at her father's shipyard in Derby. She was then quite young, and had gone out prettily attired to witness the launching of the boat. Capt. Hubbell, who, by the way, was a native of White Hills and a son of Christopher Hubbell, was just home from a cruise in Southern waters, and her pretty frock, her sunny smile and her wealth of curls attracted the sea faring man, and as he gazed on her he remarked that there was the sort of a girl that he would choose for a wife. Then Capt. Hubbell went away on another cruise, and after a few years' absence, returned to Derby town. Mary Hallock was then 18 years old, just budding into womanhood. The captain lost his heart to her, proposed and was accepted, and their union was one of happiness until death removed her husband, who his widow survived past half a century".

Abby Jane Wood married as 2nd wife Captain Benjamin Morrell and sailed with him in 1829, 1830 and 1831. During a stay in Manila, she reported the following about the American consul in her *Narrative of a Voyage to the Ethiopic, South Atlantic Ocean, Indian Ocean, Chinese Sea, North & South Pacific Ocean in the years 1829, 1820 1831* Chapter 2 page 50:

"Soon after we arrived my husband became acquainted with the American consul at Manila. A man of respectable acquirements, and of courteous manners. . . At this time as I discovered afterward, my husband began to suspect his intentions. . . The next time I saw the consul all was plain as day to me, though I dare not express myself freely to my husband, for fear of consequences from his quick sense of injury and his spirit as a brave man . . . I was fully satisfied that the consul had scattered slanders about me and my husband in order that I might feel myself so shunned and ruined as to fly to him for protection . . . During his absence I was frequently annoyed by notes from the consul, which I never designed to answer". The American consul from 1822 to 1832 was George W Hubbell.

Colonel John Steven's steamboat PHOENIX made the world's first steam powered ocean voyage in 1809. Owing to break downs and weather it took 11 days to make the 250 mile voyage. At the time, the

74

Chapter 11

future of steam propulsion was uncertain. Steam was noisy, subject to frequent breakdowns and the fuel was costly. However, as reliability improved the commercial advantages of schedules not subject to the vagaries of the wind became apparent.

Merchants during this period include a reference to the Baltimore firm of Hubbell & Pattison, dealers in produce. Josiah Hubbell (679, 1772-1838) owned a storeroom at the Light Street wharf and in 1822 offered for sale the schooner HAMILTON & HYRAM, and in 1823 prepared the new schooner INDUSTRY, *55 tons burthen for sale*.[80]

The firm of J & G Hubbell was owned by brothers Josiah (1021, 1795-1879) and Gershom E. (1019, 1788-1859) Hubbell. They owned a grocery and grain business at the foot of Wall Street, Bridgeport. In addition to the store business, they conducted coasting between Boston and New York with Gershom as master. The firm built and owned five vessels. The 95 ton VIRGINIA (VIRGINIUS) was the largest schooner built in Derby by J & G Hubbell. She was built in 1833 master Gershom Hubbell. She arrived in Boston from New York 26 July 1833. She entered Baltimore 23 March 1835 from New York and arrived in Boston from New York 19 July 1835. VIRGINIA was lost on a trip from Philadelphia to Richmond, Virginia with a load of coal. The crew and Captain Gershom Hubbell barely escaped with their lives. The loss was total as they had no insurance.[81] The sloop FAME was used for J & G Hubbell's regular New York packet. She usually made the round trip in ten days.

The HOUSATONIC was the last vessel built by J & G Hubbell. She was built at Derby in 1840 and registered at Bridgeport. She was 56 tons, length 60 feet 6 inches, draft 5 feet 5 inches, beam 20 feet 6 inches with one mast, a square stern with a figurehead. Listed as masters in 1840 were Edward Hubbell (2438, 1822-1881) son of Josiah and Charlotte Hubbell. She was advertised for New York as a new and fast sailing packet, on her second voyage, she was upset on

---

[80] Baltimore Patriot: 29 November 1822, 24 November 1823, 24 6 December 1823.
[81] History of the Hubbell Family p91.

the bar of Bridgeport harbor and cost the firm $1, 500 to refloat her. Captain Hubbell was scheduled to sail on Tuesday March 9 for New York and on Saturday March 13. Josiah Hubbell named as captain 22 Aug 1843 and Captain G.E. Hubbell, and Edward Hubbell 13 May 1845. She was sold to the firm of Morford & Trubee.[82]

On 10 December 1824, Thaddeus Hubbell registered the first steamboat in Fairfield, Connecticut, the GENERAL LAFAYETTE.

There is at least one instance where slaves were transported. The shipper was Josiah Hubbell (679) of Baltimore on 17 April 1826. (See Hubbell & Pattison page 75 above.)

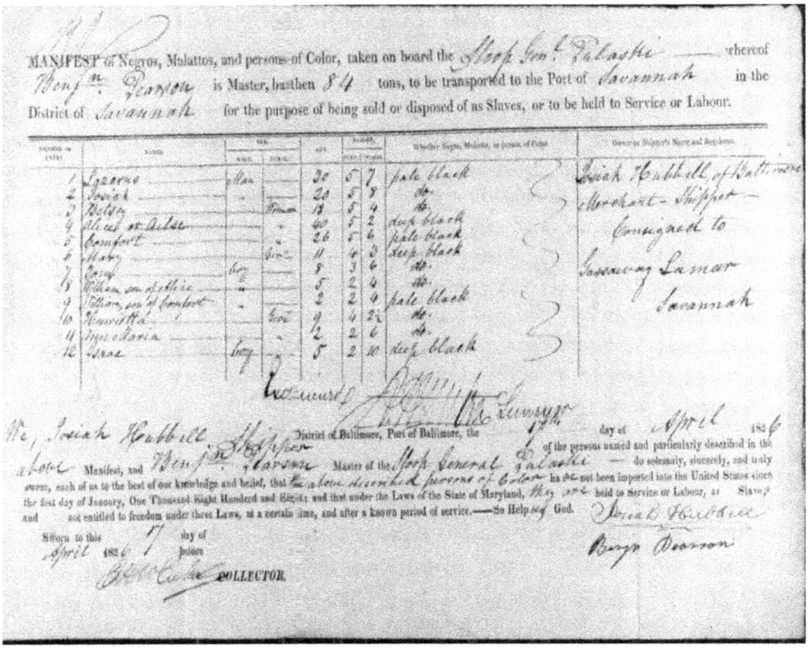

MANIFEST of Negros, Mulattos, and persons of Color, taken on board the Sloop Genl. Pulaski whereof Benjn. Pearson is Master, burthen 84 tons, to be transported to the Port of Savannah in the District of Savannah for the purpose of being sold or disposed of as Slaves, or to be held to Service or Labour.

No.	Names	Sex: Male	Sex: Female	Age	Feet	Inches	Whether Negro, Mulatto, or person of Color	Owner or Shipper's Name and Residence
1	Lazarus	Man		30	5	7	pale black	Josiah Hubbell, of Baltimore Merchant - Shipper Consigned to Gazaway Lamar Savannah
2	Josiah	"		20	5	8	do.	
3	Betsy		Woman	18	5	4	do.	
4	Alice or Ailse		"	40	5	2	deep black	
5	Comfort		"	26	5	6	pale black	
6	Mary		Girl	11	4	3	deep black	
7	[illegible]	Boy		8	3	6	do.	
8	William son of Alice	"		5	2	4	do.	
9	William son of Comfort	"		2	2	4	pale black	
10	Henrietta		Girl	9	4	2½	do.	
11	[illegible]		"	2	2	6	do.	
12	Isaac	Boy		5	2	10	deep black	

District of Baltimore, Port of Baltimore, the 17th day of April 1826

We, Josiah Hubbell Shipper of the persons named and particularly described in the above Manifest, and Benjn. Pearson Master of the Sloop General Pulaski — do solemnly, sincerely, and truly swear, each of us to the best of our knowledge and belief, that the above described persons of Color have not been imported into the United States since the first day of January, One Thousand Eight Hundred and Eight; and that under the Laws of the State of Maryland, they are held to Service or Labour, as Slaves, and not entitled to freedom under these Laws, at a certain time, and after a known period of service.—So Help us God.

Josiah Hubbell
Benjn Pearson

Sworn to this 17 day of April 1826 before
[illegible] COLLECTOR.

Figure 40. National Archives and Records Administration Record group 36 Records of the U.S. Customs Service via Ancestry.com.

[82] Ibid.

Chapter 11

Additionally, there is one instance of a slave named George owned by C. B. Hubbell of Indianola, Texas shipped to New Orleans on the S S MEXICO in January 1855.[83]

AJAX continued her China voyages, (Chapter 9). The importance of political, navigation and weather intelligence from the sea going captains can be realized by the following newspaper account of Captain Ezekiel Hubbell:

"NEW-YORK, APRIL 1823.
We learn from Capt. Hubbell, of the Ajax, from Manilla, that the British ship Mermaid arrived there on the 1st of November from Cadiz, with a new Governer for the Philipine Islands, with 240 Spanish officer to take charge of the troops at Manila and the outports. – Good discipline had been preserved among the troops since the European officers had taken command, and 5000 regulars were stationed in the city of Manilla and suburbs. . . it was the general opinion among foreigners that a great error was about to be committed by enforcing the new tariff act of the Cortes, which is 30 per cent upon all manufactured goods imported into the colonies by foreigners. . .The English East-India Company's ship Regent, from London, for Canton, struck on a coral reef, on the 18th of October . . . Capt. Hubbell states that he made his outward passage up the Palawan Coast one week after the Regent was lost, and owing to a strong S. W. current setting out of the Soole Sea, South of the Island of Palawan, fell in with Royal Captain Shoal at midnight, bore up, wore ship, hauled off 3 leagues, and lay by till daylight. The Ajax bore up for this passage off Pulo Condore, on the 27th of October, having met the strong N. E. Monsoon, and arrived off Manilla Bay on the 7th of November making the passage from Pulo Condore to Manilla in eleven days . . . He says that he would always give this passage the preference after the 10th of October, whether bound to Manilla or Canton, rather than hazard the loss of time up the regular passage late in October." [84]

The ship SABINA was built in New York 1823 and registered March 1823. She was 412 tons, length 116 feet 6 inches, beam 28 feet 10 inches. Ezekiel Hubbell, master, made his last two voyages in SABINA. She cleared Philadelphia for Havana 14 May 1824 and 17 June 1825 she cleared New York for Manila. She was reported in port Manila in November 1825 and arrived in New York 5 May 1826

---

[83] Wikipedia.ORG. Indianola, Texas is now a ghost town, wiped out by hurricanes in 1875 and 1886.
[84] *Haverhill Gazette*, published as *Salem Gazette* 2 May 1823

with a cargo of sugar, indigo, wax, hides, bark, and dye wood. He also brought back from Manila his son Henry Wilson Hubbell after an absence of five years.

SABINA cleared New York 13 December 1826 via Savannah to Lima and Pata in Peru. He obtained cocoa from Guayaquil, Ecuador, sandal wood from the Sandwich Islands and sold them in Manila. She arrived in New York 27 April 1828 with 340 cases of Manila Indigo. This was Ezekiel Hubbell last voyage.

Henry Wilson Hubbell (1344, 1806-1884) was a successful merchant who travelled extensively in pursuit of his mercantile business. In April 1828 at age 21 he arrived in New York from Manila on the SABINA, April 1830 from Canton on the SABINA, November 1831 from London on the CAMBRIA, April 1833 from Canton on the SUPERIOR and April 1835 from Canton with his brother Alexander Hubbell (1347, 1813-1840) from Canton with two Chinese servants, Ahhu and Acgui. By 1880 he was a retired merchant living at 123 East 23rd Street in New York City.

"I have retired from going to sea, some five or six years but to give you some idea of my travels, I have traveled 245,000 geographical miles since I passed my fourteenth year, which distance was made up in eight voyages to the Indies which average over 30,000 miles each voyage. . ."[85]

The packet sloop ANNAWON is the only recorded vessel from Salem, Massachusetts under the command of a Hubbell.

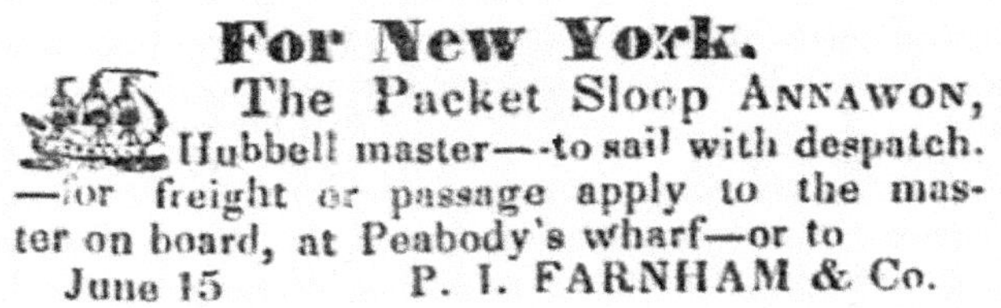
For New York.
The Packet Sloop ANNAWON, Hubbell master—to sail with despatch.—For freight or passage apply to the master on board, at Peabody's wharf—or to
June 15 P. I. FARNHAM & Co.

Figure 41. *Salem Gazette* 15 June 1832, Early American Newspapers. op. cit.

[85] History of Stratford, p 618.

Chapter 11

Also in Salem 1831 was Captain Jonathan Godfrey scheduled packet sloop ANNAWON for the Union Line at Peabody's Wharf. Jonathan Godfrey was married in 1823 to Eliza Hubbell (1378) daughter of Aaron Hubbell (534).

The sloop FLIGHT was built in 1833 at Bridgeport, registered there from 1833 to 1834. She was of 59 tons, length 61 feet 8 inches, draft 5 feet 4 inches, beam 21 feet 9 inches, with one mast, a billet head, and a square stern. William L. Hubbell is listed as master.

The brig CALVIN cleared Charleston for Wilmington, North Carolina August 1835 and then to Baltimore, finally arriving in New York, October 1835.

The third EAGLE was a sloop under the command of Gershom E. Hubbell that sailed from Bridgeport to Boston and New York with cargoes of sugar, rum, fish and plaster from 1822 to 1830 with occasional trips to Salem. On 17 September 1823 she ran ashore in thick weather near Hog Inlet, Long Island and got off with no damage. December 7, 1830 she lost both anchors off Dutch Island Light and to prevent going ashore cut the mast away between Beaver Tail and Point Judith, she was towed into port.

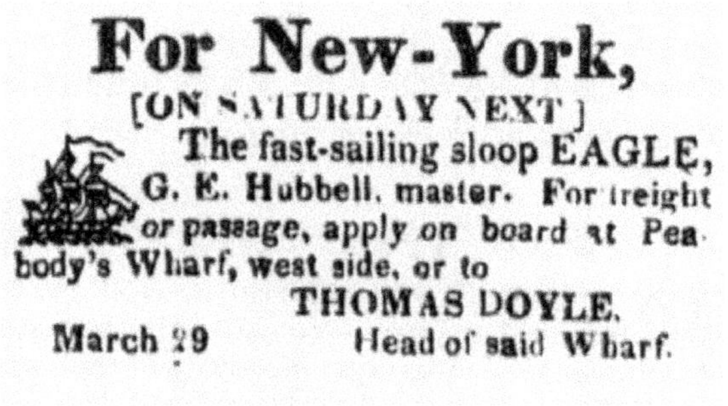

For New-York,

[ON SATURDAY NEXT]

The fast-sailing sloop EAGLE, G. E. Hubbell, master. For freight or passage, apply on board at Peabody's Wharf, west side, or to

THOMAS DOYLE,

March 29   Head of said Wharf.

Figure 42. *Essex Register* 29 March 1827. Early American Newspapers. op. cit.

IMPORT of Derby was a sloop built at Smithtown, New York in 1829, registered at Derby, Connecticut in 1831 and enrolled at New York 20 October 1829. She was 64 tons, length 58 feet 9 inches, draft

Chapter 11

6 feet 5 inches, beam 20 feet 6 inches, 1 mast, square stern, and a billet head. John Hubbell was master in 1829. In 1830 and 1831, she was a regular packet sloop from Charleston to Wilmington carrying cotton and naval stores. During February 1831 her cargo from Wilmington to Charleston was 200 bushels of rough rice, 140 barrels of turpentine and 5 bales of cotton. She arrived in New York from Wilmington, North Carolina 1 May 1831 and returned to Wilmington on 7 May. She made the trip again arriving in Wilmington the week of 14 May. In the fall of 1831 she made a round trip to St. Augustine, Florida.

Schooner HUSSAR is only mentioned once completing a trip from Wilmington, North Carolina to Charleston, South Carolina in one day, master Hubble. She carried 2200 bushels of rough rice, flour and naval stores, arriving in Charleston 6 February 1829. Possibly confused with IMPORT.

The schooner/sloop ATLAS sailed from New York to Norfolk, Virginia in October 1829 and from Savanna, Georgia to New York in April 1830 with a cargo of cotton.

A single trip for the schooner GLIDE is recorded arriving in New York from Boston 19 November 1836.

The schooner TRIAL arrived in New York from St Jago de Cuba 9 November 1832 and cleared for St Jago de Cuba 20 November 1832.

The RAPID, type unknown was in port at Port au Prince 11 October 1824 from New York via Jamaica.

The schooner THORN of Pensacola, Florida was built at New Brunswick, New Jersey in 1821. She was 48 tons, length 59 feet, beam 19 feet 6 inches, draft 5 feet with a single deck, two masts, a square stern and a billet head, Her master was Julius Hubbell 11 October 1823.

Chapter 11

The sloop INDUSTRY (3) was possibly built in Fairfield 1794. She was 58 tons with 1 deck, 1 mast and a square stern. She was registered 16 May 1796 in Fairfield. The INDUSTRY cleared New York for the West Indies on 25 September 1824 and noted in the Turks Island 21 November. She returned to Boston 3 December and was in Newbern 18 December 1824.

The brig LIMA made at least 5 trips from Philadelphia to Havana in 1824. The wide variety of cargo and customers can be seen in the list below.

"IMPORTS – FOREIGN

Havanna, brig Lima, Hubell	
Sugar 38 boxes, coffee 50 bags, segars a quanity.	*J Turner & Co*
Do 11 boxes, wax 8 Bales	*J F Oll*
Otto of roses 1 box	*Wale & Morris*
Sugar 33 boxes	*P Cruise*
Mdge 21 bales	*L D Carpentier*
Do 53 do	*Barie & Laguerenne*
Wax 18 packages	*Luke & Chew*
Coffee 15 bags, sugar 2 bbls, segars 11,000, limes 1 bbl,	
pineapples 2 dozen, preserves 4 boxes, olives 1 keg.	*F Silva*
Segars 28,000	*J M Wright*
Do 22 half boxes	*J Melizet*
Do 2 do do	*H Lelar*
Do 2 qr do white sugar 4 loaves	*L Roberts*
Limes 15 bbls	*Captain*
Old copper soda machines 2	*L Roberts"[86]*

The schooner HORATIO cleared Philadelphia 29 December 1824 bound for Lisbon. She was in Champachy in July 1825 and arrived at Wilmington, North Carolina on 10 August. She cleared on 24 August for Philadelphia where she arrived on 8 September.

The schooner RENOWN made the New York to Wilmington, North Carolina run at least 6 times from September 1831 to October 1832. She appears again in April 1836 arriving in New York from Boston.

---

[86] *Aurora General Advertiser* 7 August 1824.

Chapter 11

PARAGON of Bridgeport was a sloop registered at Bridgeport from 1822 to 1835. She is described as 69 tons, length 52 feet 8 inches, draft 5 feet 10 inches, beam 21 feet 6 inches, 1 mast, square stern and a billet head. The owners were Benjamin C. Hubbell 1822, Charles B. Hubbell 1824, Joseph W. Hubbell 1822 & 1825, Gershom E. Hubbell & Josiah Hubbell 1826, William L. Hubbell 1833. Only one reference was found. She left New York 12 December 1819 with 50 passengers and later was struck by lightning. Fortunately, no one was hurt.

The sloop Paragon Capt. Hubbell, which left here on Sunday morning, for Bridgeport, with upwards of 50 passengers, most of them women and children, was struck with lightning about 4 o'clock in the afternoon, The fluid struck the topmast and descended the mainmast, taking out a large piece nearly the whole length, and entered the hold, where it shivered two of the stanchions. Providentially none of the persons on board were injured, thought several felt the shock; and the consternation naturally excited by the occurrence, was in a great measure relieved by the excellent conduct of the captain, who displayed a remarkable presence of mind, and was thereby enabled to allay the fears of his timid passengers.[87]

The schooner THREE SALLYS of Philadelphia was built at Great Egg Harbor, New Jersey 1310 and registered June 1815. She arrived in Philadelphia from Tenerfe 22 March 1823 after sustaining damage in a storm with a cargo of wine. She cleared Philadelphia 9 April 1823 for St Jago arriving 16 May, New York arriving 12 June and arrived at the Lazaretto 19 June 1823. She was in Havana 26 August 1823 and Bordeaux in October. December 1823 she cleared New York for Brazil. In April 1824, the HERMAN of Baltimore, Captain Bradford was scheduled to leave Rio de Janeiro with Captain Hubbell late of THREE SALLYS, a passenger. In Salem 25 April 1824 the THREE SALLYS was condemned.

"Put in under Old Point, in distress. – Schr Three Sallys, Hubbell 45 days from Teneriffe, with Wine, bound to Philadelphia – 28th ult. in gale in the Gulph Stream, became water-lodged, and was very near sinking. – 1st inst while lying too (sic) under balanced reefed top-sails, sprung a leak; the sheathing coming up long side, was compelled to keep the pumps going, - Put into this as the nearest port, to repair damages. Whilst water lodged, 28th ult. saw a bright sided Brig, about half a

[87] *Daily National Journal* 18 August 1827.

Chapter 11

mile to windward, which in the space of 15 minutes after the Gale abated disappeared, supposed she went to the bottom".[88]

The brig STATIRA was 165 tons built in 1832 at Chatham, Connecticut. She was enrolled in New York 5 December 1832. From April to December 1833 she sailed from New York to Wilmington, North Carolina. She arrived in New York 30 December 1833 with a cargo of cotton and naval stores, she had split sides from severe weather and had lost part of her deck load. April 1834 she cleared New York for Vera Cruz, June she cleared New Orleans for New York with a cargo of sugar and Molasses. November she arrived in New York from Wilmington with a cargo of cotton and naval stores.

Schooner SUPERIOR arrived in Philadelphia from Vera Cruz 30 November 1827 with a cargo of specie and cochineal. In April 1828 she arrived in Philadelphia from Havana and cleared in May for St Thomas. She was at Laguira in June and arrived Philadelphia 1 September 1828.

VOLANT, a sloop was in the river at New Orleans 29 July 1823 having just sailed from Mobile, Alabama.

The packet schooner AMELIA (2), Cleared Washington, North Carolina for St. Thomas January 1826 and after 6 days returned to Washington. That same year, she made two round trips to Philadelphia with 20,000 feet of 1 ½ inch flooring boards.

The BALTIMORE, a schooner out of Philadelphia was at St Jago May 1823 and in port Amsterdam September 1823.

The PACIFIC was a schooner cleared for Murfreesboro from New York 23 July 1821 to 1823. She was last noted in 15 January 1824 when she arrived from Baltimore to New York in distress with a cargo of cotton.

---

[88] *Baltimore Patriot* 16 January 1823

Chapter 11

The ROVER was owned by Joseph W. Hubbell and registered 23 *August 1834, 17 Sept 1836 and 26 November 1839.*

"Captain Carnes, of the brig Eros, arrived at Baltimore, fell in on the 16th instant, with the schooner Pacific, Hubball, from Ocracock, N.C. bound to New-York with a signal of distress flying. Found the schooner leaky, and both pumps choked, a quantity of peas having worked into them. The crew had been for some time bailing the water out of the cabin which was four feet deep. Remained near for some hours, when Captain C. was informed the schooner was sinking, then blowing a gale, sent on board and took off 24 bales of cotton, part of her deck load. In doing this, the Eros's boat was stowed being then in lat. 36, long 76 and the schooner much lighted, concluded to bear up for Cape Henry in company, and arrived at Baltimore together. The schooner having three feet water in her hold. Captain Hubbell and crew toiled nearly a week, wet and without rest the whole time."[89]

Schooner WILLIAM ROSCOE was built at Derby 1834. She was length 81 feet 6 inches breadth 9 feet 11 inches height 24 feet with 2 masts. From October to November 1834 she traded between Baltimore and New York.

The sloop SUSAN cleared Savanna 8 January and arrived in New Orleans 5 February 1823 from Savanna.

The schooner EXIT was built in 1828, of 45 tons she was enrolled in New York 23 October 1828. One voyage is recorded under Captain Hubbell from which she was cleared at New York for Richmond.

The schooner CARDINAL arrived in Boston from New York 4 May 1840, cleared Boston for New York 29 April 1841 and again entered in Boston 22 May 1841. She arrived in Newport, Rhode Island 25 June 1841 from Pittsburg and in Philadelphia from Bridgeport 10 August 1841 She was seen again in Newport from Bridgeport 21 September 1841 and in Boston 31 October 1841.

The brig PRESIDENT MANNING was built in Providence, Rhode Island in 1822 and enrolled at New York 9 October 1824. She travelled from New York to Wilmington in 1825.

---

[89] New York Spectator 30 December 1823.

Chapter 11

The sloop COMMODORE HULL was built in Derby, Connecticut 1824 and registered 1824, 1827 to 1828. She was 45 tons, length 58 feet , draft 4 feet 6 inches, beam 21 feet 4 inches with one mast and a square stern. Joseph W. Hubbell was listed as master in 1824. By July 1825, the COMMODORE HULL was under the command of Captain McColly.

The schooner ORRA MARIA of 99 tons was built in 1822 at Steuben, Maine and enrolled 24 May 1823. She sailed from Edenton, North Carolina to Demerara on 13 May 1824.

The COMMODORE JONES was a sloop built 1835 in Derby, registered at Stratford, Derby, Westport, and Bridgeport. Her description was 69 tons, length 64 feet, draft 5 feet 9 inches, beam 22 feet 10 inches with a square stern. Reuben J. Hubbell was her master in 1835.

The schooner SOPHIA of Philadelphia arrived in Philadelphia from Havana 4 July 1826. She cleared Philadelphia for Havana and capsized 15 August 1826.

"Lost in the Gulf Stream 15 Aug 1826 Capt and crew picked up by Schooner AMELIA. Dutch Schooner AMELIA Capt. Antonio with Capt Hubble & crew of Schooner SOPHIA lost Gulf Stream 15th inst. Lat 31 Long 73 wreck, from Philadelphia for Havana capsized night of the 15th in a white squall brought exhausted crew on board by a rope."[90]

"PHILADELPHIA Aug 29 –
Arr sch Amelia, Antonio, 28 days from Jacquemel with Hache wood. Passengers, captain Hubble, and crew of the schr Sophia, which was lost in the Gulf Stream on the 15 inst. . . Capt Hubble takes the opportunity expressing his gratitude to captain Antonio, for his humane conduct in relieving him and his crew from their perilous situation and for his kind treatment while on board of his schooner".[91]

Tragic news was all too common regarding the vessels and crews that manned them.

---

[90] *Baltimore Patriot* 30 August 1826
[91] Ibid

Chapter 11

"Eaton's Neck Light House, L.I.
3 March 1845.
Another Wreck-Discover of Dead Bodies.
Dear sir:- A schooner and a sloop came down in company this morning; at 10 A.M.
one of them, supposed to be the schooner, capsized, Soon after a schooner bore
away for her, and apparently took off her crew. The wreck then drifted with a North
West wind toward the Smithtown beach. The cook of the ill-fated Reeside – a
mulatto named Cave- was found abreast of this, in five feet of water, and buried on
the point, in the "Wrecking Burying Ground." Another body, thought to be that of
Hubbell, the mate of the same unfortunate vessel, was found on Wednesday night.
He had large dark whiskers-the print of an anchor on his left arm, and that of half
an anchor on his right. He appeared to be about thirty years of age.[92]

"SCHR REESIDE. . . a letter for H. Davis, dated Feb 11, in the vicinity of the
wreck of the schr Reeside, hence for New York, . . The crew seven in number had
not been heard of: Their names as far as know, were John T. Langley, master;
Aaron Hubbell mate; Samuel Eddy 2d mate; Wm Carr colored man, seaman."[93]

Many of our Hubbell family stayed with wind power while others
adapted to the new steam technology.

---

[92] *The New York Herald* 6 March 1845.
[93] *The Boston Daily Atlas*, 15 February 1845

Chapter 12

Steamers, Builders and the Inland Waterways

By 1845 there were fewer and fewer references to the Hubbells and their sailing vessels. Steam propulsion was making rapid headway and a few changed over to the new "contraptions" One was Julius Hubbell (1127,1787-1837) of New Orleans. He was operating the towboat POCAHONTAS in 1831. She was built at Pittsburgh, Pennsylvania in 1826 and was 194 tons 127 feet in length, 1 deck, no masts, a square stern, a figurehead and a hurricane house on deck. From 1835 to 1836 he operated the steamer towboat, sometimes called a steam tug LION. She was built locally and was 278 tons with six boilers 2 chimneys and cabin on deck.

Perhaps the most notable steam sailing of the time was the following:

"The President of the United States, accompanied by his private Secretary, Mr. Trist, arrived at the Rip Raps on Saturday last, in the steam boat Potomac, Capt. Hubbell, from Washington. A salute was fired on his landing."[94]

"Steamboat POTOMAC Capt. William Hubbell leaves Washington every Friday evening at 3 and Alexandria at 4 o'clock for Old Point Norfolk & Richmond. Returning will leave Richmond on Tuesday morning at 6 o'clock and Norfolk on Wednesday at 9 A.M. Arrive at Alexandria and Washington Thursday morning. N Wattles Agent."[95]

John B. Hubbell (2440, 1835-1907) son of Josiah, was associated with the Bridgeport Steamboat Company. The company, founded in 1865 ran service between Bridgeport and New York. Two steamers were the ROSEDALE sold in 1904 and the NUTMEG STATE which burned to the waterline in 1897 after an explosion with loss of lives.

Not every passenger enjoyed the noisy passage on a steam vessel, still preferring sail as more "peaceful". Nor were the steamers without their disasters. The steamer ORLEANS was observed bottom

---

[94] *Farmer's Cabinet* 9 July 1833.
[95] *Daily National Intelligencer* (DC)

Chapter 12

up, her name visible on the stern. The Hubbell & Co. Olympic Circus had booked passage and was feared lost.[96]

The earliest record of Hubbells on the Great Lakes was in the *Detroit Gazette* of 30 April 1819 reported the PILOT, Captain Hubbell entered in from Miami (OH) to Detroit and was cleared for the return. The steamer COLUMBIA, Captain Hubbell was observed in the spring of 1850 on the Great Lakes steaming between Sandusky and Toledo, Ohio. In 1819 we find W. Hubbell of Ogdensburg running a forwarding and commission business from Montreal to any port of Upper Canada and the United States via the St. Lawrence River.

Perrysburg, Ohio on the Maumee River was a prosperous ship-building town. The screw (propeller – used to designate a ship not dependent on sails) PRINCETON was designed by Amos Pratt Hubbell (sic) and built by Samuel Hubbell (2529, 1809-1898). The engines were built at the Auburn, New York state prison. The PRINCETON ran the Buffalo to Chicago route. Samuel built his first vessel, a small schooner at Maumee in 1826. In 1830 he built the steamboat OHIO on north Front Street in Lower Sandusky now Fremont. He built a schooner for Sardis Birchard at the mount of Muskallong creek in 1834. A new propeller was commissioned by Spence, Moore & Dan in 1846 and Captain Samuel Hubbell was the master builder. He built SAMPSON of 250 tons in 1843, PRINCETON of 400 tons in 1845, SUPERIOR of 646 tons in 1845 at Perrysburg. The SAMPSON had 26 state rooms, a double berth on the upper deck, a gentleman's cabin and 2 steerage cabins. The steamship ANTHONY WAYNE was built in Perrysburg by Samuel Hubbell in 1837 for the Perrysburg & Miami Steamboat Company. She was a side wheeler for passengers and freight. The *Fremont Weekly Journal* of 22 July 1898 had this to say:

"Pioneer Ship Builder Dead. Samuel Hubbell, who was a pioneer ship builder on the Sandusky and Maumee rivers, died recently at his home at Princeton, Iowa, age 88 years. . . At the age of 17 Mr. Hubbell built a small schooner at Maumee. In 1830 he built the steamboat Ohio, on North Front street in Lower Sandusky (Now Fremont). . .

---

[96] *Barre Gazette*, 26 March 1852.

Chapter 12

He built the Commodore Perry, also the Princeton and many other vessels at Perrysburg, Ohio."

Figure 43. No record for an Amos Pratt Hubbell, drawing courtesy of Walter Lewis.

The ANTHONY WAYNE was 155 feet long and 27 feet wide with 27 foot high side wheel paddles propelled by 4 boilers. After ten years' service, she was rebuilt in 1847 and served an additional three years before the tragedy. On a voyage from Toledo to Buffalo on 27 April 1850 with a cargo of passengers, wine and cattle, the starboard side boilers exploded; of the 30 man crew, 11 were killed and a total of 38 people were killed or missing.[97] The wreck was discovered 6

---

[97] *Toledo Blade* 29 June 2008.

Chapter 12

miles North of Vermilion, Ohio (site of the Great Lakes Historical Society) in 2006 and is being studied as one of the earliest steam ship wrecks in Lake Erie.[98]

Figure 44. Great Lakes Historical Society.

The barge GLOVE of 280 tons was built at Maumee in 1846 by S. Hubbell and home port of East Saginaw. Formerly a propeller, the barge sank at Put-In-Bay April 1874.[99] Samuel Hubbell retired from ship building and moved to Princeton, Iowa around 1850 and started farming.

At Milwaukee, Wisconsin in 1848, Captain Hubbell had on the stocks at his yard on the Water Power, a large three masted schooner, scow-built 125 feet long and with a capacity for stowing 13,000 bushels of wheat. This may have been the 250 ton schooner NEBRASKA built in 1849 at Milwaukee by Hubbell.[100]

Another builder was Stephen Hubbell who built the brig LIVERPOOL in 1845 at Garden Island.[101]

---

[98] *Sandusky Register* 24 July 1898, *Freemont Weekly Journal* 12 Aug 1898.
[99] *Chicago Inter-Ocean*, 25 Dec 1874.
[100] *Milwaukee Free Democrat*, 21 March 1849
[101] Board of Lake Underwriters, Lake Vessel Register 1861.

Chapter 12

The steamer LEXINGTON, Captain Hubbell arrived in Louisville, Kentucky 7 July 1830 after a trip of 10 days and 2 hours from New Orleans. She delivered a cargo of mackerel, sugar, coffee, rice, molasses wine etc. and 70 deck passengers.[102]

As the west opened up for settlement, trade along the rivers commenced particularly during the Gold Rush. An unidentified Hubble traversed from San Francisco to Sacramento and return carrying supplies such as lumber for the miners and merchants. The sloop PHILIP HORN was noted from August to September 1855 making the trip in about 2 days each way. [10]

The DANIEL WEBSTER, a schooner was built in 1838 at Coxsacki, New York was registered from 1846 to 1875 at Norwich. Her description was 126 tons, length 77 feet, draft 7 feet 6 inches, beam 25 feet, with two masts, a square stern, with a figurehead. Peter Hubbell of Boston was the owner from 1846 to 1849.

The only mention of the sloop E HOLBROOK is that she sailed from Providence on 9 July 1856 for New York and returned to Providence from Coxsackie on 22 July 1856.

The schooner JULIA (1) one of the rare lake vessels was lost during a storm on Lake Ontario in November 1815 during a storm. Captain Hubbell of Oswego and about 35 souls perished, the wreck later drifted into Sudus Bay.

The sloop MARTHA ANN was built 1830 at Cowbay, New York; and registered at Norwalk from 1854 to 1856. She was 42 tons, length 54 feet, draft 4 feet 10 inches, beam 19 feet 7 inches with a square stern. Allen P. Hubbell master.

The sloop PRESIDENT travelled from New Haven and Bridgeport to Albany 1851 to 1852.

---

[102] *Daily Louisville Public Advertiser*, 9 July 1830.
[10] *Daily State Journal Sacramento*.

Chapter 12

The MERCHANT was noted from Maumee to Buffalo 8 August 1843.

The schooner METEOR cleared Philadelphia for New Bedford 17 June 1846.

The schooner ORIENTAL sailed between Philadelphia, Bridgeport and New York from September to November 1844.

Sailing ships docked at wharf
Figure 45 publicdomainvectors.org

Chapter 13

Namesakes and a Few More

A few vessels carried the Hubbell name. The *Alton (Iowa) Democrat* of 30 April 1898 referred to the schooner REBECCA W HUBBELL. The propeller steamboat H.S. HUBBELL was launched at Lorain, Ohio 15 May 1882. She was built by Brown Brothers & Co .[103] The schooner HUBBLE under Captain Weeks was observed at Richmond and Philadelphia in 1830, and the brig REBECCA HUBBELL, Captain Stanhope was noted in 1834.

Hubbell & Wade was a ship chandler firm that supplied ships from a dock behind the store. When the railroad separated the store from the water, the company, headed by Carmi Grumman Hubbell (8655, 1860-1928), sold house paint.[104]

The schooner JARVIS LYON cleared Philadelphia on 3 November 1848 bound for Boston.

GEORGE M KLOTTS, a schooner with ports of call at Bridgeport, Philadelphia, Charleston, New York and Boston hauling coal from May 1846 to April 1847. She was involved in a collision in December 1846 and retired to Bridgeport for repairs.

The schooner GEORGE W RAYMOND was built in 1865 at Bridgeport and registered at Pine Island from 1865 to 1872 and again in 1876. She was described as 30 tons, length 56 feet, draft 5 feet, beam 18 feet with a square stern, and a billet head. William Hubbell was recorded as master. In 1868 she had ports of call at Bridgeport, New Bedford and Norfolk.

The HENRY, a sloop probably built in Portland, Maine was registered at Bridgeport from 1859 to 1864. She is described as 88 tons, length 69 feet, draft 6 feet 6 inches, beam 23 feet 7 inches with a square stern, and a figurehead. Reuben J. Hubbell (2743, 1815/16-

---

[103] *Buffalo Daily Courier*, 15 May 1882.
[104] *Mason City Globe-Gazette* 22 July 1953.

1885) listed as master. She arrived in New Haven 10 August 1863 with a load of coal.

The schooner HENRY REMSON was built at Red Bank, New Jersey in 1851 and registered at Bridgeport from 1863 to 1886 and New York 23 February 1859. She is described as 107 tons, length 85 feet, draft 6 feet 2 inches, beam 23 feet with two masts, and a figurehead. Reuben J. Hubbell, master. She arrived in New Haven 30 May 1865 with a load of coal for the Canal Railroad. She returned to New Haven with coal on 17 July, 31 July, 16 September and 12 November 1865. She was in New London 6 May 1866 and sailed for Pawtucket.

JENNIE, a schooner, arrived in Bridgeport from New York in May 1897.

JOHN R WATSON was a schooner built in 1846 at Perth Amboy, New Jersey. She registered in New Haven, New London and Lyme. Her description was 135 tons, length 94 feet 10 inches, draft 7 feet 1 inch, beam 22 feet 5 inches with two masts, a square stern, and a figurehead. Reuben J. Hubbell was master in 1846. Two voyages are noted from Bridgeport to Albany on 16 October 1867 and again 12 November 1867.

The MINNIE GERTRUDE, master Robert S Hubbell (1595, 1831-1889) was built at Perth Amboy, New Jersey in 1868. She was registered at Greenwich and Norwalk Connecticut and Port Jefferson, New York. She was a sloop length 28 feet, draft 3 feet, beam 12 feet. Possibly a pleasure craft?

The schooner CHAS E NORTON from Portland was reported at Hells Gate 17 March 1871, Captain Hubbell.

The schooner R A FORSYTH arrived at New York from Stamford 16 October 1882.

Chapter 13

The SAM COLT schooner was in New York from Boston and clearing for Philadelphia 14 December 1865.

The steamer STAMFORD, Captain J B. Hubbell arrived at New Haven 4 July 1865 with 400 passengers.

The schooner WHITE ROCK was built in 1854 at Westerly, Connecticut 109 tons draft 7 feet. Her Master was Captain Hubble and she was owned by Joseph Jennings & Son, New York. The WHITE ROCK sailed from the Rhode Island ports of Providence, Newport and Pawtucket to Fall River, New York , Bridgeport and South Amboy from September 1869 to September 1871.

Chapter 13

Epitaph

For years the derelict wrecks of sailing vessels could be seen along the New England coast until gradually they disappeared ending a transportation era of adventure, profit and disaster. An important legacy that coexisted with the early growth of the republic.

Derelict sailing vessel at quay
Figure 46. publicdomainvectors.org

Annex A

CARPENTER'S SON of New York

85 tons built 1810 Swansboro North Carolina enrolled New York 25 Jan 1817.

CARPENTER'S SON, v, cg, ea	139	Schooner	Hubbell	New York	21 Dec 1816	Cleared
CARPENTER'S SON, ck	139	Schooner	Hubbell	Washington NC		
CARPENTER'S SON, ck, ef	162	Schooner	Hubbell	Washington NC	10 Jan 1817	
CARPENTER'S SON		Schooner	Hubbell	Washington NC	12 Jan 1817	Calc *25
CARPENTER'S SON, ch, cz	162	Schooner	Hubbell	New York	20 Jan 1817	Arrived*
CARPENTER'S SON, s, ch, cs, cl	163	Schooner	Hubbell	New York	25 Jan 1817	Cleared
CARPENTER'S SON	163	Schooner	Hubbell	Wilmington		
CARPENTER'S SON	772	Schooner	Hubble	New York		
CARPENTER'S SON, cg	772	Schooner	Hubble	Washington NC	14 Feb 1817	
CARPENTER'S SON	343	Schooner	Hubbell	Norfolk		
CARPENTER'S SON, s, cs, ef	141	Schooner	Hubbell	Washington	1 March 1817	Calc ***
CARPENTER'S SON, cg	141	Schooner	Hubbell	New York	4 March 1817	Arrived
CARPENTER'S SON, cg	165	Schooner	Hubbell	New York	14 March 1817	Cleared
CARPENTER'S SON	165	Schooner	Hubbell	Washington		
CARPENTER'S SON	773	Schooner	Hubble	New York		
CARPENTER'S SON, ef	773	Schooner	Hubble	Washington NC	28 March 1817	Arrived
CARPENTER'S SON	230	Schooner	Hubbell	Washington NC	12 April 1817	Calc *4
CARPENTER'S SON, cf, cs, ed	230	Schooner	Hubbell	New York	16 April 1817	Arrived
CARPENTER'S SON, cr, cs	231	Schooner	Hubbell	New York	26 April 1817	Cleared
CARPENTER'S SON	231	Schooner	Hubbell	Washington NC		

CARPENTER'S SON	143	Schooner	Hubbell	New York		
CARPENTER'S SON, cg, cr	143	Schooner	Hubbell	Washington NC	9 May 1817	Arrived
CARPENTER'S SON, ef	774	Schooner	Hubble	Washington NC	16 May 1817	Cleared
CARPENTER'S SON, cg	774	Schooner	Hubble	New York		
CARPENTER'S SON, cr, ck	195	Schooner	Hubbell	Washington NC	17 May 1817	Calc *5
CARPENTER'S SON, v, bv, ea, ef	195	Schooner	Hubbell	New York	26 May 1817	Arrived
CARPENTER'S SON	503	Schooner	Hubbell	Boston		
CARPENTER'S SON, as	503	Schooner	Hubbell	New York	11 June 1817	
CARPENTER'S SON, af, cr	241	Schooner	Hubbell	Boston	14 June 1817	
CARPENTER'S SON	241	Schooner	Hubbell	New York	14 June 1817	Cleared
CARPENTER'S SON, be	241	Schooner	Hubbell	Boston	17 June 1817	
CARPENTER'S SON	599	Schooner	Hubbell	New York		
CARPENTER'S SON	599	Schooner	Hubbell	Washington NC	3 July 1817	Arrived
CARPENTER'S SON, ef	344	Schooner	Hubbell	Washington NC	11 July 1817	Cleared *10
CARPENTER'S SON, ck	344	Schooner	Hubbell	New York	19 July 1817	Arrived
CARPENTER'S SON	345	Schooner	Hubbell	Washington NC	3 days	
CARPENTER'S SON, v, ef	345	Schooner	Hubbell	New York	21 July 1817	
CARPENTER'S SON		Schooner	Hubbell	Washington NC	21 July 1817	Calc *11
CARPENTER'S SON		Schooner	Hubbell	New York	29 July 1817	Arrived
CARPENTER'S SON, ci, cr, cz	653	Schooner	Hubbel	New York	4 Aug 1817	Cleared
CARPENTER'S SON			Hubbell	Cape Henlopen	7 Aug 1817	Spoke
CARPENTER'S SON	653	Schooner	Hubbel	Washington NC		
CARPENTER'S SON, cg	775	Schooner	Humble	Washington NC	9 Aug 1817	
CARPENTER'S SON	775	Schooner	Humble	New York		
CARPENTER'S SON	347	Schooner	Hubbell	Wilmington	16 Sept 1817	Calc **

CARPENTER'S SON, v, ck, ci	347	Schooner	Hubbell	New York	27 Sept 1817	Arrived
CARPENTER'S SON, cf, ci, cs	234	Schooner	Hubbell	New York	11 Oct 1817	Cleared
CARPENTER'S SON	234	Schooner	Hubbell	Washington NC		
CARPENTER'S SON, cg	776	Schooner	Hubble	Washington NC	10 Nov 1817	
CARPENTER'S SON	776	Schooner	Hubbel	New York		
CARPENTER'S SON	145	Schooner	Hubbell	NC	11 Nov 1817	Calc *12
CARPENTER'S SON, cg	145	Schooner	Hubbell	New York	17 Nov 1817	arrived
CARPENTER'S SON, ck	727	Schooner	Hubbell	New York	24 Nov 1817	Ad
CARPENTER'S SON	727	Schooner	Hubbell	Charleston		
CARPENTER'S SON	777	Schooner	Hubble	New York		
CARPENTER'S SON, cg	777	Schooner	Hubble	Washington NC	12 Dec 1817	
CARPENTER'S SON	146	Schooner	Hubbell	Washington NC	3 Jan 1818	Calc *13
CARPENTER'S SON, cg, cr	146	Schooner	Hubbell	New York	8 Jan 1818	Arrived
CARPENTER'S SON		Schooner	Hubbell	New York	12 Jan 1818	Ad
CARPENTER'S SON	81	Schooner	Hubbell	Wilmington	14 March 1818	Calc *14
CARPENTER'S SON, v, cf, ck	81	Schooner	Hubbell	New York	31 March 1818	Arrived
CARPENTER'S SON		Schooner	Hubbell	New York	21 April 1818	Ad
CARPENTER'S SON, v, cr, cs	235	Schooner	Hubbell	New York	26 April 1818	cleared
CARPENTER'S SON	235	Schooner	Hubbell	Washington NC		
CARPENTER'S SON, ef	600	Schooner	Hubbell	New York	5 May 1818	
CARPENTER'S SON, cg, ef, ef	600	Schooner	Hubbell	Washington NC	15 May 1818	Arrived
CARPENTER'S SON	196	Schooner	Hubbell	Washington NC	20 May 1818	Calc *15
CARPENTER'S SON, ck, ci	196	Schooner	Hubbell	New York	29 May 1818	Arrived
CARPENTER'S SON, v, cf, ck	197	Schooner	Hubbell	New York	6 June 1818	Cleared
CARPENTER'S SON	197	Schooner	Hubbell	Washington NC		
CARPENTER'S SON	149	Schooner	Hubbell	Washington NC	1 July	Calc*16

Annex A

CARPENTER'S SON, v, cg, ck	149	Schooner	Hubbell	New York	7 July 1818	Arrived
CARPENTER'S SON	779	Schooner	Hubble	New York		
CARPENTER'S SON, co	779	Schooner	Hubble	Washington NC	31 July 1818	Entered
CARPENTER'S SON, cg	778	Schooner	Hubbe	Washington NC	31 July 1818	
CARPENTER'S SON	778	Schooner	Hubbe	New York		
CARPENTER'S SON, cf	198	Schooner	Hubbell	Washington NC	12 Aug 1818	Calc *17
CARPENTER'S SON, v, bi, ck	198	Schooner	Hubbell	New York	16 Aug 1818	Arrived
CARPENTER'S SON		Schooner	Hubbell	New York	20 Aug 1818	Ad
CARPENTER'S SON, cf, ck, co	85		Hubbell	New York	29 Aug 1818	Cleared
CARPENTER'S SON	85		Hubbell	Washington NC		
CARPENTER'S SON, co, cs	87	Schooner	Hubbell	Washington NC	23 Sept 1818	Calc *18
CARPENTER'S SON, v, cf, ck, ci	87	Schooner	Hubbell	New York	1 Oct 1818	Below
CARPENTER'S SON, fu		Schooner	Hubbel	New York	2 Oct 1818	Arrived
CARPENTER'S SON, cr	734	Schooner	Hubbell	New York	12 Oct 1818	Cleared
CARPENTER'S SON	734	Schooner	Hubbell	Washington NC		
CARPENTER'S SON	236	Schooner	Hubbell	Washington NC	4 Nov 1818	Calc *19
CARPENTER'S SON, v, cr	236	Schooner	Hubbell	New York	7 Nov 1818	Arrived
CARPENTER'S SON		Schooner	Hubbel	New York	16 Nov 1818	Ad
CARPENTER'S SON, v, ck, cs	199	Schooner	Hubbel	New York	22 Nov 1818	Cleared
CARPENTER'S SON	199	Schooner	Hubbell	Washington NC		
CARPENTER'S SON	735	Schooner	Hubbell	Washington NC	31 Dec 1818	Calc*20
CARPENTER'S SON, cr	735	Schooner	Hubbell	New York	4 Jan 1819	Arrived
CARPENTER'S SON		Schooner	Hubbell	New York	7 Jan 1819	Ad
CARPENTER'S SON, cg, cr	150	Schooner	Hubbell	New York	9 Jan 1819	Cleared
CARPENTER'S SON	150	Schooner	Hubbell	Washington NC		

CARPENTER'S SON, cs	238	Schooner	Hubbell	New York	11 Jan 1819	
CARPENTER'S SON	238	Schooner	Hubbell	Washington NC		
CARPENTER'S SON, ef	804	Sloop	Hubble	Washington NC	5 Feb 1819	Cleared
CARPENTER'S SON	804	Sloop	Hubble	New York		
CARPENTER'S SON, ci, cs	151	Schooner	Hubbell	Washington NC	1 March 1819	Calc *21
CARPENTER'S SON, cg, cr	151	Schooner	Hubbell	New York	8 March 1819	Arrived
CARPENTER'S SON	651	Schooner	Hubbel	Charleston	5 March 1819	Cleared
CARPENTER'S SON	651	Schooner	Hubbel	New York	15 March 1819	Ad
CARPENTER'S SON, v	218	Schooner	Hubbell	Charleston SC		
CARPENTER'S SON, ax, cs	218	Schooner	Hubbell	New York	19 March 1819	cleared
CARPENTER'S SON, ck, co, cr	731	Schooner	Hubbell	New York	22 March 1819	Cleared
CARPENTER'S SON	731	Schooner	Hubbell	Washington NC		
CARPENTER'S SON, v, cs	220	Schooner	Hubbell	Washington NC	21 April 1819	Calc*22
CARPENTER'S SON, co, cr	220	Schooner	Hubbell	New York	27 April 1819	Arrived
CARPENTER'S SON		Schooner	Hubble	New York	4 May 1819	Ad
CARPENTER'S SON	244	Schooner	Hubbell	Washington NC	12 June 1819	Calc *23
CARPENTER'S SON, cr	244	Schooner	Hubbell	New York	16 June 1819	Arrived
CARPENTER'S SON		Schooner	Hubbell	New York	30 June 1819	Ad
CARPENTER'S SON, cr	245	Schooner	Hubbell	New York	5 July 1819	27
CARPENTER'S SON, cs	153	Schooner	Hubbell	Washington NC	17 Aug 1819	Calc *24
CARPENTER'S SON, cg, cr, ef	153	Schooner	Hubbell	New York	23 Aug 1819	Arrived
CARPENTER'S SON		Schooner	Hubbell	New York	25 Aug 1819	Ad
CARPENTER'S SON	154	Schooner	Hubbell	Washington NC	6 days	
CARPENTER'S SON, cg, cr	154	Schooner	Hubbell	New York	7 Oct 1819	Arrived 15

* Naval stores anchored since Friday quarantine ground.

Annex A

Naval stores for P & C W Davenport & Co.

** Naval stores & cotton.

15. 6 days naval stores. Capt Hubbell died Marine Hosp Staten Island 8 Oct 1819.

27. Returned to port, high winds.

*** 4 days naval stores, flax seed, tobacco.

*4 4 days naval stores

*5 9 days naval stores

*10 9 days

*11 8 days naval stores

*12 6 days naval stores

* 13 days naval stores and flaxseed

*14 17 days naval stores and staves.

*15 9 days naval stores and furs

*16 6 days naval stores

*17 4 days naval stores

*18 9 days naval stores

*19 3 days

*20 5 days naval stores

*21 7 days naval stores

*22 6 days naval stores

*23 4 days naval stores

*24 6 days naval stores

*25 8 days naval stores.

Note 11 Oct 1819 Capt Hubbell Carpenter's son died Marine Hosp Friday.

Annex A

Sources explained:

s	Baltimore Price-Current	ea	American Beacon & Commerical Diary (VA)
v	Baltimore Patriot	ef	City Gazette & Daily Advertiser (SC)
af	Repertory (MA)		
as	Columbian Sentinel (MA)		
ax	Boston Gazette		
be	Boston Daily Advertiser		
bi	Boston Patriot		
bv	Providence Gazette		
cf	Columbian		
cg	Commercial Advertiser (NY)		
ch	Courier (NY)		
ci	Daily Advertiser (NY)		
ck	Evening Postg (NY)		
cl	Exile (NY)		
co	Mercantile Advertiser (NY)		
cr	New York Daily Advertiser		
cs	National Advocate (NY)		
cz	New York Price-Current		

Transcription of a letter to George W Hubbell in Manila,

George W Hubbell Esq   Canton
12mo.24.1829
Manila

Dear Friend
The enclosed letter by thy Brother Henry makes us commercially acquainted, it was
my intention to have written at some length, but most of the American Ships being
on the eve of sailing, it only allows me to state in general terms . . . the English East
India company have made a demand on the Alice Roy of this place for a general
charge in the . . of condemning the foreign commerce of this Port, the declaration
(?) Was made some three months since & the Alice Roy has informed them that
such change is totally inadmissible with the Laws of this Country, and they are now
completely at issue. The suspension of so large a portion of the trade was expected
early in the season to have had the effect particularly to reduce teas to very low
rates; but so far from realizing such an expectation, higher prices have been paid ..
than the last season for young Hyson, other green have also been high; but as this
cause has been owing very much to our own bad management, and the stocks of all
teas except young Hyson excessive there can be no doubt but that if the companys
Ships should not enter the Port that are shall have teas at less hire?, say in the
second month & this month then we have before seen & I ma of the opinion that
ships arriving here in those months will stair. A very good chance of obtaining
freights at reasonable rates to the U. States; vessels coming for that purpose from
Manila should bring a cargo of Rice to save to save them the Port charges & if any
of thy friends come this way for that or any other object it will at all times give me
much pleasure to afford them assistance and I shall expect that thee will make use
of me. The suspension of the companys trade has had only a slight effect on British
Cotton Goods, Shirtings 38 @ 40 yds by 354@36 inch wide of pretty fair quality
are worth about $7 & $7.25 per piece, Cambric Muslins 12 yds by 45 inches of a
good quality are worth $2.60, inferior 41 &42 in $1.60 & $2 per piece, Hand . of
printed goods of all kinds are very dull, American made white & brown shirtings
will not bring their cost in the U. States – Enclosed is a price current. If thee should
be disposed to visit china, if it will give much pleasure for thee to make thy home
at my Factory.
With much respect
I am your friend
Siging, at Dunn
Sent via Macao by Hez(?) Hubbell

Annex B

George W Hubbell Esq   Caonton 1 mo 16.
1830

Dear Friend

I avail myself by the U. States ship the Vincennes to say that the Hon: the E.E.I. Companys demands on this government have not yet me with the slightest concession and the prevailing opinion appears to be that they must wait for further instructions from England; which may require eight months from this. Their ships have rec? orders from the committee to prepare for sea with ten days provisions on board; and the impression is that they will proceed to Manila to remain perhaps for some months. We are also informed that two or three of the ships are preparing for the Yellow Sea with a petition for the Emperor; and as they will have a head wind & current may be three months before they can hear of the reception it meets with. From these circumstances, I am induced to believe that it is reduced to a certainty that Teas will be very less in the course of two months hence – the quantity shipped to the U States this season amounts to

19,765	chests	young Hyson
6,937	"	Hyson
11,646	"	H. Skins
3,830	"	Tonkays
4,018	"	Gunpowder & Imperials
1,100	"	Bohea
11,850	"	Souchong
118	"	Pecco
59,264	"	in the following vessels say

1829

Ship Tobacco Plant	sailed 10mo15		for Philada
" Mentor	"	" "	Boston
" Sabina	"	12mo24	New York
" Milo	"	" 26	Boston
" Fanny	"	" "	Philadelphia
" Ajax	"	" 28	New York
" Panama	"	" 29	"
" Sumatra	"	" "	Salem
" Globe	"	" 30	Phila
	1830		
" Liverpool Packet	"	1mo4	Boston
" Franklin	"	1mo4	New York
Brig Melville	"	1mo6	Baltimore

There remains in Whampoa
Ship Isabella expected to sail in all the 4th month
"   Israel

105

Annex B

" Emerald   to sail in two or three weeks
Brig Twofriends[105]

---

[105] Mystic Seaport Library.

ANNEX C

From the Philippine Philatelic Journal.

Peele, Hubbell and Company (American)
1822-1887[106]

The American firm of Peele, Hubbell an Company is believed to the earliest foreign (non-Spanish and non-Asian) business house in Manila. Prior to establishing permanent residency on the Islands, the Hubbells made several visits, presumably to determine if a business house would be economically feasible. In 1817, Captain Ezekiel Hubbell of Bridgeport, Connecticut, went to Manila aboard the *Citizen*, representing the firm, Hoyt and Tom and Company. He did not stay, however, but returned to New York with a load of sugar and indigo valued at $10,000. In 1819, he returned to Manila on the *Citizen* with his son, George William Hubbell, as supercargo (officer on the ship in charge of the cargo). Again, both returned to the United States. These trips convinced the family that a profitable trade could be established between Manila and the United States.

In March 1821, George William Hubbell married; and in April, sailed with his father, Ezekiel Hubbell, and brother, Henry Wilson Hubbell aboard the *Ajax* to Manila, arriving in August 1821. The conclusion of the third trip to the Philippines resulted in the formation of the firm, George W. Hubbell and Company, in Manila the following year. George W Hubbell was president and Henry W Hubbell served as a clerk in his brother's firm. This firm, the progenitor of Peele, Hubbell and Company, commenced business and issued its first commercial circulars on January 1, 1822. The Hubbells have the distinction of being the first Americans to permanently reside on the Island.

Using ships and shipping connections of their father, Ezekiel Hubbell this firm successfully traded Philippines goods to the United States and Europe. By 1823, the firm was already exporting sugar to South America, and doing increased business with the United States, particularly to firms in New York and Salem. Between 1825 and 1827, George W. Hubbell spent time in the united States promoting trade with Manila, resulting in increased trade with the Philippines.

George W. Hubbell died on May 3, 1831, at the age of 35. His brother, Henry W. Hubbell, then assumed control of the firm. Since Henry W. Hubbell was in Connecticut when his brother died, the business in Manila was directed by John McAuley, the senior staff member of the firm. Also, in 1831, Henry W. Hubbell formed a new partnership with J. W. Peele of Salem, Massachusetts. J. W. Peele

---

[106] "History of Four Major Business Firms and Their Mail from the Spanish Philippine Period: Peele, Hubbell, and Company (American) 1822-1887", Don Peterson, PPJ, First Quarter 1992, Vol. XIV, No. I, Page 9.

arrived in Manila aboard the *Sapphire* in May 1832. On July 1, 1832 circulars were issued announcing the formation of the new firm, Peele, Hubbell and Company. Under the leadership of Henry W Hubbell, an increased effort was made by this firm to improve trade between the Philippines with England and China.

J. W Peele and John McAuley resided in Manila while Henry W. Hubbell sailed about the world on ships owned and chartered by his father and other New England ship owners. In 1834, Henry Hubbell retired and was succeeded by Henry Lawrence of New York. In that same year, Ezekiel Hubbell died. J. W Peele and Henry Lawrence retired in 1843. From then on, although the firm's name remained the same, the principal partners resided in Salem.

The earliest postal history of this firm is known by a forwarding agent handstamp. Rowe (1984) reports the use of a forwarding agent handstamp by Peele, Hubbell and Company in Manila on mail to, or from, or passing through Manila, between 1834 and 1841. The oval handstamp measures 40 by 17 millimeters, is either black or red, and contains the words, "Forwd' by Peele, Hubbell & Co. Manila." It is considered rare. My records show that this handstamp was in use as late as 1844.

Peele, Hubbell and Company in Manila acted as a forwarding agent for mail to and from other business firms and private individuals in the Far East at that time. According to Rowe (1984), a forwarding agent is "a person, or firm, who undertakes to see that the goods or correspondence of another are transported without himself acting as the carrier."

TERMS

aft	toward the stern
alum	aluminum potassium sulfate used as a styptic and in dying and tanning
beam	the width of a ship
beat down	sail against the wind?
boom	a spar along the bottom edge of a rigged sail
bowspirit	a spar that extends forward from a ship's bow
brig	2 masted vessel, square rigged on both masts
careen	to heal over or to list, to lie on one side for cleaning
Cassin	possibly related to cassia, an aromatic bark
celestial navigation	
	navigation by observing the position of heavenly bodies
china root	Probably from the Chinaberry tree, for medicinal purposes
cordage	ropes, lines, hawsers used in the rigging of a ship
draft	the depth to which a vessel is immersed
foremast	forward most mast
foresail	principal sail on a foremast
fustick	a tropical wood
hogshead	usually 63 gallons but can be as much as 140 gallons
indigo	dark blue dye from the indigo plant
lignumvitae	a hard wood used for blocks
main mast	usually the tallest mast on a ship
main sail	principal sail on the main mast
nankins	Chinese blue & white porcelain
picul	133 ½ lbs.
pipe	varies but usually 4 barrels, 2 hogsheads or 126 gallons.
puncheon	varies but usually 80 gallons.
schooner	fore and aft rigged sails, two or more masts, after mast tallest.
ship	3 or more masts, all square rigged.
sloop	single mast, fore and aft rigged with a bowsprit.
spar	a pole
supercargo	One in charge of the cargo, a person employed on board a vessel by the owner of the cargo to sell the merchandise at ports and to buy and receive goods for the return voyage.
tierces	1/3 of a pipe about 42 gallons

BIBLIOGRAPHY

Albion, Ralph, *The Rise of New York Port 1815-1860*, Hamden CT: Archer Books, 1961.

Albion, Robert G. et al. *New England and the Sea*, Mystic: Mystic Seaport Museum, Inc., 2004.

Bolles, Albert Sidney, *Industrial History of the U.S: From Earliest Settlements to the Present Times*.

Bown, Stephen R., *Scurvy*. New York, St. Martin's Griffin, 2003.

Brewington, Marion V., *Maritime Philadelphia 1609-1837*: Offprint from *The Pennsylvania Magazine of History and Biography*, April, 1939, Kessinger Publishing.

Clowes, Laird, *Sailing Ships, Their History and Development*: London, Her Majesty's Stationery Office, 1962.

Danforth, Ardath, *Perrysburg Revisited:* Fostoria, Gray Printing, 1992.

Dow, Francis, George & Robinson, John, *Sailing Ships of New England 1607-1907*: New York, Skyhorse 2007.

Druett, Joan, *Rough Medicine*: New York, Routledge, 2000.

Francaviglia, Richard V. *From Sail to Steam 4 Centuries of Texas Nautical History* 1500-1900.

Gilje, Paul A. *Liberty on the Waterfront*: Philadelphia, University of Pennsylvania Press, 2004.

Homberger, Eric, *The Historical Atlas of New York City*: New York, Henry Holt, 1994.

Howay, A List of Trading Vessels in the Maritime Fur Trade 1795-1804

Hunter, Douglas. *Half Moon, Henry Hudson and the Voyage That Redrew the Map of the New World*: New York, Bloomsbury Press, 2009.

Kaminkow, Marion & Jack, *Mariners of the American Revolution* Genealogical Publishing Co., 1967.

Knapp, Lewis G., *Stratford and the Sea*: Charleston SC; Arcadia Publishing, 2002.

Knight, Frederick Edward, *Over-Seas Britain*: London, John Murray, 1907.

Larbaree, Benjamin, et al *America and the Sea: A Maritime History*: Mystic, Mystic Seaport Museum, Inc.,1998.

Lavery, Brian, *Ship The Epic Story of Maritime Adventure*, DK Publishing, 2008.

Mallory, Mary, *Boston Men on the Northwest Coast*.

Marx, Robert F., *Shipwrecks in the Americas*: New York; Dover, 1987.

McKay, Richard C, *South Street A Maritime History of New York*: New York; Haskell House,1934

Millar, John Fitzhugh, *American Ships of the Colonial and Revolutionary Period:* Norton, 1978.

Miller, R., *The New York Coastwise Trade* (1865-1915)

Morrell, Abby Jane, *Narrative of a Voyage to the Ethiopic & South Atlantic Ocean, Indian Ocean, Chinese Sea, North & South Pacific Ocean in the years 1829,1830, 1831*; New York: J J Harper 1833

Orcott, Samuel, *A History of the Old Town of Stratford and the City of Bridgeport, Connecticut*: Tuttle, Morehan & Taylor.

BIBLIOGRAPHY

Orcott, Samuel, A *History of Old Town Derby, Connecticut:*Press of Springfield Printing Co, 1880

O'Shaughnessy, Andrew Jackson, *An Empire Divided – The American Revolution and the British Caribbean*

Partridge, Helen, *Easton – Its History*: Collingsville CT;Lithographic, Inc. 1972.

Peterson, Don, *History of Four Major Business Firms and Their Mail From the Spanish Philippines*, Philippine Philatelic Journal 1:1/9

Roosevelt, Theodore, *The Naval War of 1812*: New York, The Modern Library, 1999.

Weeden, William B, *Economic & Social History of New England* 1620-1789.

Works Progress Administration, *A Maritime History of New York:* Doubleday, 1941.

INDEX

INDEX

INDEX

INDEX

INDEX

116

INDEX

www.ingramcontent.com/pod-product-compliance
Lightning Source LLC
Chambersburg PA
CBHW020913090426
42736CB00008B/619